C000101643

A Passion for Mountain

Sail and Flight

A Passion for Mountain

Sail and Flight

Barry Cliff

Copyright © 2013 Barry Cliff
All rights reserved

First published 2008
2nd edition 2013
3rd edition 2019

Photographs are copyright and reproduced by kind
permission of the copyright holders, who are acknowledged
where appropriate.

Published by Barry Cliff, Elbeck Cottage, Litton BD23 5QJ
Tel: 01756 770207

Printed by Pioneer Press Ltd., Skipton

Typeset in 11/16.5 Garamond by Typescript, Giggleswick, BD24 0DJ

*Frontispiece: B Cliff (left) and R Baillie on
Table Mountain, Cape Town, South Africa
(Photo: M Mamacos)*

Table of Contents

		Page
Author's Notes		viii
Biographical notes		xii
Foreword		xvi

Chapter 1   Mountaineering   20
Early Days102Agriiculture; The Alps; Studies; Kenya

Chapter 2   Mount Kenya   36
The 1st attempt; A Different Christmas;
The 2nd attempt; Tragedy on the Mountain;
The Firmin-Hicks route; The West Face;Thompson's Flake;
Equatorial Winter Sports; Glacier Flying

Chapter 3   Nelion's north-east pillar and east face   66
The pillar; The east face

Chapter 4   Kenya Independence   82

Chapter 5   Mount Kilimanjaro to Mount Kenya
           in under 24 hours   90

Chapter 6   An epic with John Cleare   102

Chapter 7   Crocodile Encounter   108

Chapter 8   Adventures in Aviation 1   116
Early days; Crop spraying and the Accident

Chapter 9   Adventures in Aviation 2   134
de Havilland Rapide; Guyana; Bush Flying;
Operation "El Dorado"

Chapter 10   Adventures in Aviation 3   157
Crop spraying in the UK and Return to Kenya
safari flying; Seychelles; Return to University;
World Health Organisation and River Blindness;
The Wayen accident

Chapter 11   Sailing Adventures   178
National Service; Annette; Sunstream; Batian

Chapter 12   The Atlantic   194
To South America; Georgetown, Guyana – again;
Repair and Return across the Atlantic

Chapter 13   The Canaries   216
To Gibraltar; Madeira; and the Canaries;
The End of Batian

Chapter 14   St Helena   228

Chapter 15   Epilogue   234

Acknowledgements   242

List of Illustrations   246

Author's Notes

The first publication of "A passion for mountain, sail and flight" was in 2008.

I attempted to persuade book publishers in London to undertake the publishing and selling of the book but in spite of sending them the manuscript, I was not successful. As a consequence, I was eventually obliged to self publish with a local printing firm.

A fine review of the book with photographs (including one of Indiana Jones!) was published by the Yorkshire Post on September 11th 2008 and another review was published in the Weekly News on January 3rd 2009, also with a comparison to Indiana Jones! The publicity resulted in a rapid sale of the copies I had printed at the local premises and it was soon "sold out".

There have been numerous requests for a copy of the book which regrettably I have been unable to fulfil. Also, work colleagues and friends of mine who are aware of some of my escapades and adventures have reminded me of some of the events which were missed out on the first publication. I have been persuaded to write more and publish this, a second edition, with other perhaps more graphic inclusions of events.

Intreresting comments on the first publication included:
"even though I spent many years climbing and doing a bit of adventuring, your story makes me feel like a wimpy couch potato" ... a climber

"I always feel that I have been rather fortunate to survive to my present age but on reviewing the hazards you encountered in your life time I have to hand it to you as the premier survivor of all time" ... a climber

"I have bought copies to give to people with similar aspirations but with more limited lifestyle" ... a climber/sailor

"When I first met this rather quiet man at Devil's Bridge my first thoughts were that you were probably a retired solicitor, or someone of that type, who had spent most of their working life in an office, WOW was I wrong!!!" ... a motor cyclist amongst others, Kirkby Lonsdale

Early on in life I had decided that I wanted a life of adventure and I have strived for that. Quotations of the newspaper reviewers of the book which I feel are particularly relevant are "... some people used to call me fearless though I prefer senseless - the fear was never there. I was good at sensing danger and knew how to deal with it long before others did", "... bush flying is less predictable than airline flying. I have to rely completely on myself and that suits me very well and if I make a mistake, it's on my own head. I like that!" (Observer colour supplement, 27 February 1972).

A local lady, on reading the first edition, advised me to "never to invite me to come on an adventure with you because you've killed all your friends off!" It's true I have lost many friends on the way but I don't quite see it as she does and I don't feel I have caused the demise of valued friends and colleagues.

Barry Cliff, Litton 2013

Biographical notes

Roy Smith, Associate Professor
Bloomsberg University, PA USA
2008

Barry Cliff

From the Yorkshire moors near to where he was born to the Sahara and beyond, this travelogue of one man's journey takes us to places few of us will ever see. It is an unforgettable long odyssey of remarkable journeys and tragedies as an accomplished alpinist, ocean sailor and bush pilot on three continents.

On graduating from Leeds and Cambridge universities, he joined the British Colonial Service and initially served as an Agricultural Officer in the waning days of the Empire. Not content with the staid life-style of a Colonial civil servant he forged his own agenda of adventure. As a mountaineer he grew in stature making the first ascent of the north-east pillar of Nelion on Mount Kenya, a fine and difficult route many had aspired to.

A testimony to the breadth of his capacity to take on something new was in 1963 when in a home-built wood and canvas canoe he attempted the first descent of the Uaso Nyiro river that runs through the home of the Samburu tribe. This might so easily have been his last adventure. I was invited to be his companion but at the last minute I received a posting to the U.K. and he had to search for another companion. After attacks by crocodiles and a damaged canoe they were forced to walk out through the thorn scrub and make contact with nomadic hunters.

We met again at Chamonix in the French Alps after he had

learned to fly. There we climbed the north face of the Aiguille Dru in good style over two days with one bivouac. Sadly it was to be Barry's last mountain for his aircraft accident was shortly afterwards.

Leaving Africa behind – for now – he travels to Guyana ferrying diamond prospectors in his Beaver float plane into remote regions of the forest and taking off from the famous Kaieteur Falls.

It seemed only inevitable, considering the formative years he spent in Africa – a continent that has captured the soul of so many of the old Colonial service – that Barry would eventually return. As an old "Africa hand" he was invited to manage the aerial operations of the World Health Organisation's River Blindness campaign in West Africa, which involved spraying the rivers by aircraft to control the parasite. Supervising a roughish collection of fixed-wing and chopper pilots from the Vietnam era he doubtless commanded considerable respect and would keep strict control.

In retirement he turns to ocean sailing with a voyage across the Atlantic in an elderly wooden boat and up the Demerara river to see old friends.

He weaves a palpable sense of excitement and a wry sense of humour into accounts of his far-flung adventures, whilst introducing us to a most unlikely and entertaining cast of characters. I feel very privileged to have been his friend and climbing partner.

Foreword

Rusty Baillie, Idaho, U.S.A.

2007

It was early 1961 and we had just come off Mount Kenya. Barry was leading me up Agags Corner, a rock-climbing route on the Lukenia cliffs, just outside Nairobi. He was tip-toeing up very small holds on a very steep rock face. He moved smoothly and carefully, with precise elegance but with absolutely no drama or flamboyance. I was beginning to see that, when my turn came to do the climb, I would receive another lesson. I had joined Barry for the difficult West Face glacier route on Mount Kenya with only a single, easy ice climb to my credit. By watching Barry like a hawk and copying the way he cut steps and used his crampons, I was able to lead my pitches without plunging us both to our doom. Now I was learning how to really rock climb. The fact that we were using some of the hardest climbs in the world as our classroom was just a sign of our youthful exuberance and carefree arrogance. We made plans to follow our luck – Cenotaph Corner, The Eigerwand, Everest …

Five years later I was again out with Barry. We had come to the Cornish coast in southern England where Barry was about to start a new job, flying tourists on ten-minute pleasure trips around Land's End in a De Havilland Rapide bi-plane. Now he was carrying my two-year-old daughter, on his shoulders, down a steep sea-cliff path. My wife and I had set up a small tent on the beach and we were kayak surfing. The fact that Barry could piggy-back Sheila in such a spot, and dare to paddle out into the crashing surf, was remarkable: he was still recovering from a plane crash that had broken his back and nearly killed him.

As the poet Burns says, "The best laid plans of mice and men oft go astray." Life Happens. The optimistic dreams of our youth face shipwreck on the Rocks of Reality. True Survivors have the wondrous ability to gather the pieces of their shattered plans and craft a satisfying and fulfilling existence from their youthful inspirations.

Then I lost touch with Barry. I got a good job, worked at being a dad, climbed when I could. Barry travelled the continents, sailed the oceans and explored the skies. We got together occasionally.

It was really only when I sat down to read the manuscript of this book that I fully realised how well Barry had kept alive his Spirit of Adventure, how hard he had continued his search for The Grail! The smiling modesty with which he had tip-toed up the "Extremely Severe" Agags Corner was still there, in the casual and understated prose. I was so glad that I had this chance, after all, to share in his later adventures. As the circle closes, it is a rare pleasure to feel that, overall, life has been quite sweet.

Chapter 1

Mountaineering

Early days

My interest in rock climbing started whilst at grammar school aged sixteen, studying first for School Certificate and then Higher School Certificate. School friends Jim Rennie, David Stead and Hugh Gordon met in the school gymnasium each lunchtime when we would cavort on the ropes and wall bars imagining ourselves as climbers and improving our arm strength. One day, Jim produced an ex-Army karabiner and with a clothes line we used it to formulate belaying and pitching climbs up the wall bars. We graduated to gritstone rock at local Almscliffe, Ilkley and Caley crags with the purchase of a hemp rope (Carr's band), and helped each other with techniques we had read about, learning to lead climbs with running belays and how to abseil. We also learned rescue techniques when Hugh got into a difficult situation whilst we were abseiling over an overhang at Caley Crags. Halfway down the abseil his brand-new sweater was sucked into the karabiner at his waist and jammed, preventing any further movement. Watching him helplessly swinging under the overhang was hilarious to the rest of us and in fear of his mother's wrath it took him some time to agree to cut the sweater out of the karabiner with the knife that we lowered down to him.

My first foray into the mountains was with Jim Rennie to Glencoe in Scotland. We were attracted to Clachaig Gully described in the guide books as the longest gully climb of 1,735 feet of mild severe climbing on "rock through jungle scenery, best done in May or early June when the wild flowers are at their best," and "to be avoided in wet weather." We climbed it in April on a warm day and can recall how we enjoyed gulping the water on the way up the gully only to find near the summit that there was a dead stag lying in the stream in a badly decomposed state! David Stead then joined me to climb Tower Ridge on Ben Nevis, but I had to leave shortly afterwards to return to the Royal Navy in Portsmouth for National Service whilst David journeyed to the Cairngorms. Soon after returning to Portsmouth I learned that David had lost his life in a climbing accident involving his party of three, which included an instructor! All had fallen together and only one, a girl, had survived, albeit badly injured.

In 1952, on a visit to Rylstone Crag near Skipton in North Yorkshire, Jim and I did a first ascent of Rylstone Wall, graded "very severe". In the 1989 *Yorkshire Gritstone Guidebook* it is recorded that, "This was the pair's only new route in England. They both made their names on big mountains in far-flung corners of the world (Jim Rennie in Antarctica)."

Agriculture

After National Service in the Royal Navy it was time to consider what profession I wished to have in life. I had been potato picking whilst at school and life on a farm really appealed. I considered that a profession out of doors and something dealing with nature would suit me. I made enquiries about forestry and agriculture and eventually visited the agricultural professor at Leeds University. There was a degree course of three years leading to a qualification of B.Sc (Agriculture) but the professor felt that my limited practical experience was not sufficient to be considered for the course. He suggested that if I was prepared to spend a year on a farm he would then look more favourably on my application for the qualification. To gain dairy experience, I got a position as a farm hand on a dairy farm at Low Bentham near Settle in the Yorkshire Dales and went up there on a motor cycle to live and work with the farmer and his family. I very much enjoyed learning and working in all aspects of dairying but after six months there felt I needed some arable experience. I was accepted on an arable farm near Driffield on the Yorkshire Wolds and spent a further six months living and working on that farm. I was then accepted for the degree course at Leeds University and duly started studying there.

Learning about all aspects of farming was interesting but after a lifetime of daily physical work, albeit getting very fit and strong, I did not settle

Eight of the students studying agriculture at Leeds University. B Cliff on right.

too well into a life of serious study. The highlight of each week was a farm visit every Wednesday to a working farm. We were a group of twelve young men, some of whom were farmer's sons but I was the only student who had completed National Service - in the Royal Navy.

23

A coach was arranged weekly to take us to the selected farm and it became a serious task when the coach turned up to persuade the driver to first take us to a pub where the drinkers would try and consume as much beer as they could get down in a short time with sometimes embarrassing consequences.

I can recall an interesting visit to a farm on the Yorkshire Wolds where the farmer was mechanising as much as he could in order to cut his labour costs. We examined combined harvesters, all types of tractor and heavy machinery. He still retained one horse and as we were about to leave, the horse which I believe was a huge Clydesdale came into the yard after a day's work with an elderly hand riding side saddle on it. The farmer called out to Jack, his elderly employee, to come over to talk to us and answer our questions no doubt already well aware of his attitude to anything mechanical. Jack was happy with his position above us on his horse but not accustomed to addressing a crowd of young men. When asked what he thought of his horse and machinery he came out with a wonderful one-liner to sum it all up in his lovely Yorkshire country accent. He said, "'osses is ah reet 'osses is", and then asked his horse to move away which it immediately did, obviously preferring Jack's company to us young men.

The Alps

Whilst at Leeds University and as a member of the Leeds University Climbing Club I went on two visits to the Alps. As a group of seven young men we travelled out by motorcycle and being impecunious we took all our own gear with us, including a considerable amount of food. Amongst the four who had motorcycles we tossed a coin to decide who should attach a "chair" (sidecar) to his bike in order to carry all the gear. First, Frank Butler had this doubtful honour and for the second trip, "Mac" Macgregor – the then President of the Club. On the first visit to the Dauphine Alps, Jack Moody was to be my pillion rider. (He was my partner on numerous routes in the Lake District.)

On our very first day in the Alps, five of us were scrambling up

The seven young men in front of the motorcycle with sidecar: Jim Pike (behind), Barry Cliff (front left), Frank Butler (front right). Frank was killed in a climbing accident in Snowdonia two years after this picture was taken.

25

a ridge, and un-roped. In the lead I used a loose rock and warned those following to treat it with care which the following three duly did. Perhaps the warning was not passed on to Jack as last man for he pulled outwards on the rock and it came away, causing him to fall with it for about 20ft. He damaged his foot and was unable to walk on it. We had to carry him back to our campsite, where it became clear that it had to be medically examined. La Berade, where we camped by the river was 20 miles or so from the hospital in Grenoble and illegally riding three on my motorcycle we took him there. His foot was X-rayed with the surgeon announcing it to be unbroken and advising him to bathe it every few hours in the glacier stream at the campsite, and to WALK ON IT! Jack duly complied whilst the rest of us climbed. The foot gradually increased enormously in size and became a deep purple colour. We were all so concerned that we made another visit to the hospital to learn that the X-ray had been mis-read. The heel bone was indeed fractured and with the damage now done, Jack was advised to fly home to England for surgery. Our suggestion to the surgeon of travel by sidecar was immediately ruled out and he talked of the patient having to be flown in a recumbent position. We could never have afforded that and by pooling our limited resources we arranged a flight home for Jack. He limps to this day and, as far as I know, has never climbed again to the same high standard and agility he possessed on the wonderful climbs we did together. The only doubtful, positive, outcome from his mishap was that he was rejected at his medical as unfit for National Service.

The second visit to the Alps was more successful and this time I had Kit Roberts on the pillion. Again to La Berade, in the Dauphine Alps, we had better, more ambitious plans. Climbing as two ropes of two, Kit and his brother Bowen Roberts, with myself partnered by David Wade, we climbed the south face of Les Ecrins in a nineteen-hour day from the same original camp site as we had used on our first visit. David Wade and I then climbed the east face of the Aiguille Dibona before he and I finished our holiday with an ascent of the south face of La Meije. Soon after our return to the U.K., David sadly lost his life, leading a party of Boy Scouts on a rock climb on Dow Crag in the Lake District.

Studies

Rock climbing became a serious passion for me and whilst reading for a degree in agriculture at Leeds University, my studies began to suffer from spending too much time on rock. I barely scraped a pass but the Colonial Office was sufficiently impressed to offer me a position in Kenya with initially one year's study at Cambridge followed by a year at the Imperial College of Tropical Agriculture in Trinidad before then proceeding to Kenya. Study at Cambridge was with a group of thirty agricultural graduates from other universities and was to lead to a Diploma Agriculture (Cantab.). To my astonishment we were told that we would all be expected to take the exams at the end of the year but however well we fared in the exams three people would not qualify for the Diploma (Cantab.) award due to poor degree results from

27

"red-brick" universities. With my bare pass from Leeds, my name came up first and there and then it seemed rather pointless to be too serious about studying. I joined the College Boat Club and rowing replaced climbing since there is a dearth of rock in the Cambridgeshire area.

In an excuse to get to the hills and given the choice of a subject for a dissertation I chose "Hill Grazing" which gave me the opportunity to visit the Isle of Skye where I was already known to the farmer, Mr McRae, at Glen Brittle, the climbing centre for the Cuillin Hills. After the first term of rowing each afternoon it was necessary to get some material for my dissertation so in the Christmas vacation Mike Dixon from Leeds joined me on my motorcycle for a winter ride up to Skye. Our intention was to attempt to make the first winter traverse of the Cuillin Ridge and after an epic ride on ice-covered roads we were pleased to see the ridge covered in snow and ice. In excellent weather conditions we traversed the first half of the ridge from Sgurr Alisdair and spent a long time getting over the inaccessible pinnacle, heavily coated in ice. Soon after that we bivouacked in an icy corner for the first half of a very cold night. At 02.00 the temperature suddenly changed and a warm, westerly wind started to blow off the Atlantic. By morning all the snow and ice had gone and wet through we descended back to Glen Brittle, clearly unable to claim our adventure as a complete winter traverse. (It was done two years later by Tom Patey, MacInnes and party, by which time I was already in Africa.)

At Cambridge my best achievement was to win an oar for rowing but as anticipated, accolades from the exam results were sadly lacking. A berating at Cambridge was swiftly followed by an interview at the Colonial Office in London where I was requested to explain my poor performance at Cambridge. Fortunately the senior member conducting the panel of questioners was a rower and also apparently in sympathy with my reasoning for not being too serious about studying. Their decision was that the Colonial Office was prepared to continue with my training in Tropical Agriculture at the Imperial College in the West Indies but that if I failed the exams there I would be sacked and would be required to reimburse £1,000 for their wasted training. Somewhat chastened I crept away and with my impecunious position, determined that on no account must I fail!

The Imperial College of Tropical Agriculture in Trinidad was a wonderful place to study and I found all our lecturers fascinating and very knowledgeable practical men, most of whom had spent years abroad dealing with tropical crops. Learning from them and actually seeing the crops growing on farm visits was fascinating and I became passionate about tropical agriculture. To learn about coconuts we were taken to a coconut plantation on the east coast of Trinidad adjacent to a wonderful beach. We were instructed that the crop needs 70-90 inches of rainfall a year, and that it can be grown at coastal regions and can tolerate an appreciable degree of saltiness with the coconut itself being able to survive 110 days in sea water. Seventy trees to the acre can be planted and will produce 40-60 nuts per tree per year, taking 10-12 years to be in full production. We saw how copra (the dried, fleshy part of the fruit; the coconut oil extracted from it is collected and used largely in soap making and the remaining cake forms a good stock feed) is made, needing 7,500 nuts to make one ton and also witnessed the production of coir fibre. At some stage we asked how the crop is harvested and the manager informed us that one of his workers would be with us at the end of his day to demonstrate and in the meantime we were invited to go to the beach to have a swim. We were in the tropics and welcomed his offer. So we went to the edge of the plantation to change and get in the sea.

Eventually we were called back to the coconut trees to see the demonstration. A young man appeared carrying a length of rope made into a sling which he proceeded to place around his ankles. His agility was quite amazing and he shot up a

coconut tree with a cutlass between his teeth and cut down some coconuts to fall amongst us. We were told that a good man could climb and harvest 60 to 90 trees a day. My fellow students turned their attention to me and announced, "Cliff, you reckon to be a climber let's see you do it!" I accepted the challenge and bare foot,

B Cliff climbing the coconut tree

30

clothed only in swimming trunks and a tee shirt I approached the arena which they formed round the tree which they considered suitable! Spurning the rope sling, I climbed it in a layback position (rock-climbing term) using the leaf scars as foot holds with my bare feet and got to about 15 feet before attempting the descent in the same position. Much more tricky than the ascent since I had difficulty in seeing the leaf scars from above. Undoubtedly much better and safer to use a rope sling round the ankles as did the manager's employee!

I worked hard and negated the £1,000 debt hanging over my head with a good pass of the Diploma in Tropical Agriculture. In preparation for Kenya, one of the lecturers even taught me basic Kiswahili (*lingua franca* of East Africa) which he had learned in his position as an entomologist in East Africa.

During the Easter vacation the Imperial College arranged a week's visit for us 30 students to then British Guiana in South America to see sugar cane and rice growing on the coastal area and once there, a flight was also arranged into the interior of the country to see cattle ranching. At the airstrip (a rough piece of land called Atkinson Field) we were told to walk over to a battered looking DC3 aeroplane standing in a corner of the field. We wandered across to find a trestle under the port wing with a man standing on it and his head buried in the engine. We called to him and covered in oil and grease he looked down with some distain when we informed him that we were waiting for the pilot to fly us into the interior. From his lofty perch he calmy said, "I AM the pilot." It was to make a lasting impression on me and we were to meet much later in life when he worked on my own aeroplane. The man, as I later learned was none other than the famous Harry Wendt in the country who started Guyana Airways when the country became independent, then flying a Grumman Goose seaplane.

In the DC3 when we were told to board there were no proper seats but only two long benches along the sides of the fuselage. There were also signs of cattle having been his previous freight. We flew into the Rupununi savannah in the interior to a very rough airstrip and waiting for us there were a number of horses with Amerindian cowboys all smiling at this new fresh pink meat, most of us in shorts! Few of us had ever been on a horse but we were told to select our mount and "Get on". The cowboys had been anticipating their fun and as soon as we mounted they slapped our charges and away we went ... most of us out of control! Saddles were not provided for they were far too tough for such things and the cowboys all rode bareback! Most of us went the length of the airstrip before getting control and managing to turn around. We were in a very sorry state with the skin rubbed off from the inside of our legs and one or two were unable to walk! Two were even later requiring medical attention. The cowboys were hysterical with mirth at these soft white men. Nevertheless we had a very interesting tour and it sparked my ambition to eventually search for a similar life style.

Kenya

Of course I had read all about Kenya and in particular Eric

Shipton's book, "Upon that Mountain", had inspired me and in great anticipation I was flown out to Nairobi, together with one other student who was from a Scottish university and the Imperial College, also destined to be an Agricultural Officer. At the airport we were met by the Agricultural Department and each put into a Land Rover which contained a tent, camp table, and a chair and told that we were expected to spend time "on safari" in the course of our work. I was delighted and even more so when told I would be posted at the foot of Mount Kenya, to a rice research station on the Mwea plains. The Scotsman, remarking to me that he "had never slept in a tent" was destined for Nyzanza way to the west of the country. I never saw him again.

At the research station I was told that Mt Kenya could be easily seen from there but in the present rainy season it would be some time before it became visible. I looked for it in vain every day for a month before very early one morning it appeared shining like a great jewel in the sky above cloud to the north. Leave was not possible with my new work and I became impatient with attempts to get nearer and hopefully set foot on the mountain. Private transport was required and in a brief visit to Nairobi by hitchhiking I purchased a motorcycle (a BSA Star Twin 500cc) and planned to ride to the mountain at the first opportunity. Whilst in Nairobi I visited the Mountain Club of Kenya and persuaded one of its members to visit me and ride up the forest track on my motorcycle in an attempt to get to the moorland above the forest. He did visit me at the rice research station for a weekend and we made our attempt.

My first view of Mount Kenya from the Rice Research Station

The bike was a handful on murram (non-tarmac) roads and with a passenger, even more difficult. We left the bike halfway up the track and managed to walk to the moorland where we passed a cold night under a large boulder. Early in the morning we had a wonderful view of the main peaks, whetting my appetite even more to climb on them. At the bike there had been rain and we cautiously slid back down the track. With the throttle closed, and hence without much noise we very nearly hit a buffalo which shot across the track in front of us! I asked Tony Nield, a Kenya-born man, if he had seen it. "Barry, man", he said, "don't ask me to come with you again." It was the start of my many adventures on that beautiful mountain and it became a very valued part of my life.

Chapter 2

Mount Kenya

"Kenya possesses them, it can awe the most truculent soul, stir the mean ones to resent its majesty, and it can mean the very poetry of life to the appreciative few who can respond to its splendour."

Behind God's Back, Negley Farson

The first attempt

In yet another visit to Nairobi to attempt to meet other climbers, I stayed at the Y.M.C.A. hostel where the warden told me of a climber who lived there. I was introduced to Tony Rowland who worked as a quantity surveyor in the same firm as Tony Nield. He had climbed in England and we managed to have a day's climbing together at Lukenya, a practice crag only forty-five minutes drive from Nairobi. Don Gray, another quantity surveyor with the same firm and also a climber joined us and we had an enjoyable day on warm red granite-gneiss.

I mentioned my intention to climb on Mount Kenya as soon as I could get some leave and learned that Don Gray also had the same ambition. Some time later and with a week's leave available we made our attempt to climb the normal route to the summit, Batian. Taking two porters from Raymond Hook's farm to help carry all our gear we climbed across the moorland and camped beneath Midget Peak on the south side from where the porters descended. The next day we climbed the Lewis Glacier to Top Hut with the intention of going to the summit the following day. Don was struggling on the scree but we passed a good night in the hut and he felt he was fit enough for the long climb to Batian. We left the hut at daybreak to cross the Lewis Glacier and at 07.00 and climbing solo we started the easy scrambling to the more serious rock. At the foot of Mackinder's Chimney we roped up with Don offering me the first lead. At the top of the chimney I belayed and prepared for him to climb. He appeared to be having some difficulty and once he was alongside me, announced that he

Don Gray at the top of Mackinder's Chimney – he became unwell soon after this picture was taken

was feeling unwell. Within ten minutes he was coughing blood and it was obvious that there was no question of continuing.

It was a struggle to get down and in his distressed state it took us some time to reach the tent where a further problem awaited us. All our gear, including food and sleeping bags was missing, obvi-ously stolen by the porters who must have waited around until we went further up the mountain. Clearly we had to get off the mountain and it took all day to reach the road head. Some way before, whilst we were resting on a fallen tree I heard a noise and looked up to see a rhino about thirty yards away looking at us and sniffing the air. I immediately warned Don, his only comment being, "Barry, I couldn't care less!" He was certainly unable to run and fortunately the rhino eventually disappeared into the bush. Further down I called at the first farm to find Beryl

Markham (the first person to fly solo east-west across the Atlantic in 1936, described in her book, "West with the Night"). She kindly drove us down to Naro Moru where we arranged transport to Nairobi. Don was hospitalised and never climbed again, but he did recover. Later I visited Raymond Hook's farm with the police and they were given permission to search our two porters in the local village. Our equipment was found under a bed in their huts and told to strip by the police, one of the porters was found to be wearing my underpants! Clearly poverty-stricken I felt so sorry for them that I requested no charges be made.

A Different Christmas

by Tony Rowland

It was over the Easter of 1958 that six of us from the Y.M.C.A. set out on a first expedition to Mount Kenya. We left Nairobi early on Good Friday distributed between a saloon car and my sturdy short wheel-base Land Rover.

All personnel plus camping and climbing gear squeezed into the Land Rover at Naro Moru Police Post and were soon on the forest track heading for the moorlands and lower slopes. We delayed only momentarily whilst a herd of buffalo crossed the track just ahead of us and we were soon disgorging people and equipment at the Meteorological Clearing, at ten thousand feet, where the Land Rover was to be left.

Leaving the forest track we trekked up the very steep marshland until we reached the easier gradient and path through the giant heather and lobelias of the upper moorlands. Our view ahead was totally restricted because of cloud clinging to the slopes. This was still the situation as we pitched camp at the head of the Teleki valley at an altitude of 13,500 feet. Our journey from

Nairobi had started at a height of 5,200 feet and we were all pretty breathless as we coped with tent erection and fire lighting.

As night wore on the clouds lifted ro reveal a star-strewn canopy of singular beauty. Outlines of the mountain's peaks were just visible on the border of sight.

The entrance flap of my tent faced the mountain and as the early sun stirred me into activity, I took in the view ahead. The sky was a cobalt blue and unfettered by a single cloud but pierced by two rock and ice spires. These peaks being supported by a base of rock cliffs and glaciers, the whole emerging from a wide area of glacial morain.

If ever a vista could inspire a wish for intimate involvement then this was surely it.

And so it lead to Christmas when, now four of us, set off to climb this staggeringly beautiful mountain. John and Ken from the Njoro Plant Breeding Station joined Barry Cliff, an agricultural officer and an accomplished climber, and myself all met up at Naro Moru on Christmas Eve.

We got off to an inauspicious start as Barry had managed to close the door of his Land Rover onto his hand and damage two fingers. With blood slowly oozing under the nails, he - stoically - elected to carry on and check the situation as we got higher up the mountain.

We reached Top Hut, at 15,000 feet after a single day's slog but Barry had a very uncomfortable night and was obviously suffering. We decided to "operate". By heating a needle on a Primus stove we pierced the nails of his damaged fingers to attempt to release the blood but it did not ease his pain and he finally accepted that he was in no fit state to climb. He offered to remain in the hut whilst I attempted to persuade our other two colleagues to accompany me in a summit bid.

It was with some reluctance that John, who had some climbing experience, agreed to come as second on the rope and we, thus, set off across the Lewis Glacier, as dawn was breaking on Christmas Day.

It was an immaculate day with dry and firm rock. The first six or seven pitches were technically undemanding but it was still with a feeling of great satisfaction that we gained height in the champagne atmosphere of that early morning. Rounding Mackinder's Gendarme we were faced with Shipton's Crack, the crux move of the Normal Route.

In the event it went smoothly and we were now set for the summit bid. After a few hundred feet of straightforward climbing we were on Nelion's summit and in glorious conditions. So good, in fact, that a light aircraft was able to climb to our 17,000 feet perch, circle and the pilot to wave to us.

Now, the dilemma as so frequently encountered on a climb of this nature, was whether there was time to cross the lateral distance, involving descent and crossing of the Gate of the Mists, to Batian and return and descend off the mountain in safety. If Barry had been able to climb it would have been only too easy but this was not the situation. So, it was with a very heavy heart that I had to abandon the idea of proceeding to Batian and return to my companion and commence our descent.

Roping down was a slow procedure with the many belays and the frequent untangling of rope snags. As it was we only just completed the final abseil as the light faded.

Barry and Ken awaited us at the foot of the climb with a hot drink and with the sustenance downed we trudged back across the

Lewis well-satisfied with our day and that we had taken correct decisions.

Top Hut might not appear to be the greatest place for Christmas celebrations but ours were not muted as we thoroughly enjoyed the uniqueness of the Time and Place.

Tony Rowland

The second attempt

My next opportunity to get on the mountain for a few days was to be again with Tony Rowland who was recovering from a bout of malaria and expecting some sick leave. Following my request to the Agricultural Department to be transferred from research work to extension work I was allocated an area in the African reserve where I would be dealing directly with African farmers to improve their farms and introducing cash crops in an advisory capacity. I felt more attracted to this work than that of research. My new posting was even closer to the mountain – an African village on its eastern slopes (Runyenjes, north of Embu). Here a house was made available for me with a view of the mountain from the bedroom! It was immediately necessary to learn Kiswahili and an increment to my salary was withheld until I had passed the required examination. It was varied and interesting work and I enjoyed the close relationships I developed with farmers sympathising with and understanding their struggles to make a living in difficult circumstances.

I myself lived close to nature and at the end of a day's work I would often go down to the Tana River to swim. There were two other European men living in the village: a Land Consolidation Officer with whom I got on well and an Administration Officer where a strained relationship developed. His attitude to me was that I was one of his staff under his control as District Officer and should report to him. I was shaken to receive a letter one day which read, "It has been brought to my notice that the agricultural officer has been swimming in the crocodile infested Tana River. This will cease forthwith." I felt it was an intrusion into my private life and an unnecessary way to inform me. Of course I was aware of the crocodiles but it was not the only time I came across the hierarchy that colonial administrative officers often imposed upon usually highly qualified technical staff working in the areas that the former felt was under their control. I continued to swim in the Tana!

At my house I employed a male cook called Muchiri from the Kikuyu tribe. For the large garden I employed a "shamba boy" (gardener) called Njeru also Kikuyu. Njeru was a young man aged twenty who had come to my house one day seeking work. He had been a member of the Mau Mau uprising, living for two years in the forest surrounding Mount Kenya. He was a very fit young man who showed an interest in rock climbing and I invited him to accompany me to local crags I found in the area where I taught him rope techniques as we climbed.

The Mau Mau movement was a secret subversive movement, mainly within the Kikuyu tribe which came to light following the shooting of Chief Waruhui outside Nairobi on 7th October

1952. A few days before his death he had condemned Mau Mau and his murder was the terrorists' reply. Following more violence, a state of emergency was proclaimed throughout the then colony of Kenya. The Mau Mau movement brought bloodshed to Kenya in what appeared to be a rejection of colonial rule and western ways. There were atrocities and attacks at isolated farms. Many Kikuyu became willing converts yet others had to be dragged to the Mau Mau oathing ceremonies. Of all the tribes in Kenya, the Kikuyu had the greatest respect for the binding power of both secular and magic oaths. These ancient oaths and ceremonies were distorted and perverted by the Mau Mau leaders and helped to bind the bulk of the tribe together in the support of Mau Mau and to turn the tribal mind against civilisation. In theory Mau Mau was anti-white, but in practice the terrorists killed a hundred times as many Africans as Europeans. The days were usually peaceful but at night the terrorists swept over the reserve and settled areas, taking food, money and life. The security forces were often baffled by the problem of what to do next but so were the terrorists. They had no coherent plan of revolt and the objective was hazy. The Mau Mau answer was to take to the forest, the traditional hiding place of the tribe. There were many instances of bravery and courage amongst those fighting the Mau Mau in the forest with the eventual ending of the emergency in 1955.

With Tony Rowland's forthcoming sick leave I was able to take some time off work and we decided to make an attempt on the north face of the mountain (Firmin-Hicks route, done in

1944, and still awaiting a second ascent). I suggested that, rather than going on one of the normal approach routes, we could go direct from my house up through the forest onto the moorland and then follow one of the valleys up to Top Hut. Tony agreed and with Njeru's knowledge of the forest I decided to take him with us and also two other friends of his, as porters.

The forest on the eastern side of Mount Kenya is extensive and the Urumandi area comprises large tracts of bamboo on a horizontal plateau where we promptly got lost. We were not even certain that we were progressing uphill and hearing animals crashing about in the vicinity was particularly unnerving. Njeru suddenly stopped and calmly said, "Just here we built an elephant trap when I lived here." He led us a few yards to the left and sure enough there was the old elephant trap, rather overgrown. He of course knew exactly where we were and we had no further problem locating the moorlands where the porters and Njeru left us to continue whilst they descended, arranging to meet us at a cave in the valley we were in, in seven days time. With now augmented large loads, Tony and I continued up to Top Hut. After resting for a day we then walked round to the north face and erected my one-pole tent actually leaning against the rock of the first pitch on the route. We had a poor night's sleep and Tony clearly felt weak after his malaria. Nevertheless, he offered to take the first lead and at 06.15 we were ready for off. Off it was, for at fifteen feet up the route Rowland promptly fell off, landed on the tent and broke the pole. It was an inauspicious start and we decided to abort the attempt. We didn't climb the mountain and still in both Rowland's and my memories is the hunt for the cave and the porters in heavy mist and rain. The porters and Njeru were wide-eyed and astonished to see two "mzungus" (white people) coming out of the mists and exactly on time! Chastened again we descended back to my house.

My time in Kenya had started in 1957 by which time the country was peaceful. Njeru refused to talk of his time in the forest, or of Mau Mau and I respected his silence. He was a good companion on our various adventures, very tough and reliable but he let me down in the end. With his constant questioning me, "What was the summit like?" I dearly wanted to take him to Batian and bought him the necessary gear including an expensive pair of boots. Once he was suitably equipped he disappeared with all I had bought and sadly I never saw him again.

Amongst the giant heather on Mt Kenya moorland. Njeru in front, Tony Rowland behind

In an attempt to meet more of the Mountain

Club members I arranged a weekend party at my house for the whole club. As an incentive I also offered to arrange the catering and provide food. I had met a hunter in my work area and admired his skill with bow and arrow. I asked him if he could get me a warthog (wild pig) to which he promptly agreed. The day before the weekend we constructed a spit in the garden and roasted the warthog. It was delicious white meat, not unlike tender chicken and everyone congratulated the cook. Some time later in an opportunity to get to Nairobi and attend a club night I got a rather unwelcome reception! A number of people from the party had contracted a tapeworm and my bush pig was the main suspect!

Mount Kenya from the south

Tragedy on the mountain

Whilst living in Runyenjes the Land Consolidation Officer, John Longhurst expressed a desire to go on the mountain for a weekend and George Neame, an agricultural assistant also living and working with me had similar aspirations. With the struggle Tony Rowland and I had experienced in the forest on the last attempt, we decided to drive round to Naro Moru on the west side and climb the recognised Naro Moru track to Top Hut and from there climb Point Lenana (the third highest peak of Mount Kenya and an easy ascent). It all seemed feasible and we left very early on Saturday morning, drove round to Naro Moru and up the track in George's Land Rover as high as we could get before hiding it in the forest. (It was a Government Land Rover and was not intended for private use!)

We were all fit and we managed to arrive at Top Hut at 16.30. In the hut there were three residents – Spyratos (Greek), Kalkbrenner (German) and Annemarie Weber (Austrian) who informed us that two of their party – Straubinger (Austrian) and Levy (son of a Kenyan family) had left at 04.45 to climb the mountain to the summit of Batian. At about 18.00 as the light was fading, I looked across the Lewis Glacier and saw the two climbers abseiling down alongside Mackinder's Chimney. Fearing that they were late I suggested that they would probably bivouac and wait for daylight. After our exhausting day, we then turned in to sleep. At about 20.00 a further party of three arrived – Michael Robinson, Thompson and Matthew (a guide). At 20.30 whistle blasts were heard from the mountain and I was awakened and joined the Hut party to cross the glacier where at the foot of the scree we were able to make contact by shouting to Levy who had apparently given the alarm by whistling through his fingers (he had no whistle). He was four hundred feet up and had a broken leg. He was unaware where Straubinger, his companion, was. Clearly the rescue team was required and I therefore left the Hut party and returned across the glacier to the Hut to arrange for someone to start down to Naro Moru for help. George Neame, a tough cockney and rugby player was the fittest and immediately offered, together with Matthew to run down the track in the dark with a report I wrote for the police station at Naro Moru. Then joined by Robinson and carrying sleeping bags, a hot drink and a collapsible stretcher we found in the hut, we re-crossed the glacier and rejoined the Hut party. We all climbed the scree to the start of the route and soon afterwards found Straubinger's rucksack. In searching at the foot of the climb I then found Straubinger's body and determined that he was dead.

Kalkbrenner, Robinson and Annemarie Weber returned to the Hut where they found that the runners had returned as the hurricane lamp they were given kept going out. They were given a torch and set off down again at about 01.00. Moonrise would be about 03.00 but it was a formidable task to ask anyone to go through the game-infested forest in the dark. Meanwhile, and in the dark, Spyratos (who had no experience of rock climbing) and I climbed towards Levy. At the foot of Mackinder's Chimney we were able to talk fairly easily with Levy, another one hundred feet above us and where he courageously said that he was safe and alright and could last out the night where he was. It seemed best then to leave Spyratos there to keep in periodic verbal contact with Levy whilst I returned to the Hut to rest, with the intention of returning at dawn to climb up to Levy with supplies and first-aid equipment. At 04.30 and helped by Robinson and Kalkbrenner we re-crossed the glacier and Robinson and I managed to reach Levy soon after dawn at 07.00 where we splinted his leg and managed to lower him ten feet to a larger ledge. We only had a short piece of rope and with the pain he suffered on movement were unable to move him further.

Meanwhile, the runners had reached Naro Moru police station at 06.00, a tremendous feat and the rescue operation was then put into place. Michael Robinson and I then spent the rest of the day with Tony Levy before we witnessed the rescuers starting to arrive at Top Hut as dusk was falling. We spent a reasonable night with Tony quite warm and comfortable in two sleeping bags. The first of the rescue team reached us at 09.30 the following morning where they injected morphine into Tony and prepared to lower him. After helping with the preparation and with more rescuers then arriving, Michael Robinson and I then descended to Naro Moru, where, amongst the crowd Tony Levy's mother approached and asked us if we were the two men who had been with Tony. She thanked us profusely and I told her that

Tony was in good shape and being carried down the mountain. Immediately I had spoken, someone tapped me on the shoulder and called me to one side with the devastating news that Tony had just died at the lower Klarwill's hut. He had apparently never regained consciousness after the morphine injection. Since Michael and I had spent so long with Tony, we had learned what a fine courageous young man he was and it was a great privilege to have been able to help him in his last hours. Even now fifty years later I have difficulty in coming to terms with his tragic death.

The Firmin-Hicks route

A few months after that accident, the Agricultural Department transferred me to the Nyambeni Hills on the north-east side of Mount Kenya. The hills are separate from the lower slopes of the mountain and in spite of being in the northern desert area, are sufficiently high to be lush and green with a good rainfall. It was anticipated that tea could be grown successfully and I was expected to try it. As a start I planted six bushes in my garden, which easily thrived on the one hundred inches of annual rain that fell in the village (Maua). Thereafter twenty African farmers were selected and issued with tea seedlings for a small plot each. Teaching the farmers how to grow and harvest tea as a cash crop was fascinating work. Close neighbours were the Adamson family (George and Joy) further down the plains, but their lioness (Elsa) gave some concern to some of the farmers on the lower slopes of the hills.

A letter arrived from a climber friend of mine from university (Jim Pike). He had graduated in Chemical Engineering at Leeds two years after my degree and he had accepted employment in the oil industry in the Arabian Gulf. With no mountains there and limited facilities in his leisure time he was clearly not content. In replying about my situation and possibilities in my "paradise" I suggested he should come to Kenya. To my surprise he got the next aeroplane and joined me in my African village where I had been issued with a fine house. He did not seem too concerned about looking for work and was quite content to assist me with mine. Of course we planned to go on the mountain and at the first opportunity we attempted the north face, first climbed by Arthur Firmin and Peter Hicks in July, 1944 – and the route Tony Rowland and I had planned

Top of Firmin's Tower - Jim Pike climbing

to do! Ours was to be the second ascent (25th August 1960) sixteen years later. The third ascent was only one week after ours. Starting at 06.30 we reached Batian, the highest peak at 12.15, and were back at the tent before dark at 18.00. These days it is regarded as the normal and easiest route on the north side of the mountain.

Jim Pike left me soon after that to accept a lecturing appointment at Nairobi College before then going south to South Africa. Knowing that he would be visiting England I suggested that he called to see my parents, living only a few miles from his own. Our friendship and respect for each other as climbers then went considerably further. At my home he met my sister, working abroad in Rome and just visiting. He wrote, "I've known you and climbed with you for ten years and never even knew you had a sister." They eventually married and now have a herb farm run with their family in New Zealand.

The West Face
My next opportunity on Mount Kenya was when Michael Robinson and Annemarie Weber (both from the accident) and I took leave to celebrate Christmas on the mountain. The three of us climbed the normal route to Nelion and Batian before Annemarie left us to return to her work. Michael and I then climbed the south face route to Batian and descended by the normal route we had climbed two days previously. I was anxious to climb the wonderful West Face and whilst returning to Two Tarn hut we came across a group

of South Africans from Cape Town University camping beneath Midget Peak. They had been on the summit by a number of difficult routes and were clearly competent climbers. Their leader was Rusty Baillie who we had seen cutting steps high up on the Diamond upper glacier. Michael had felt apprehensive on the Diamond when we crossed it on our south face climb and he had already expressed his reluctance to tackle the West Face. I mentioned this to Rusty Baillie who immediately offered himself as a partner. He quickly packed his gear and accompanied us up to Two Tarn hut.

Rusty and I left the hut at 02.45 and made our way to the foot of the West Face. I was somewhat shaken when we sat to put on crampons and Rusty suddenly said, "How do you put these things on?" Notwithstanding, he soon demonstrated his strength and skill and we climbed the first glacier, the Heim, by moonlight in one hour. Dawn was breaking as we crossed the gap between the two hanging glaciers and then we encountered hard ice on the Forel. It took us five hours of step cutting to reach the head wall where we traversed to the right for one hundred feet and took to the rock. After two pitches and some verglas we reached easier rock, and climbed onto the summit of Batian at 14.00. We traversed the Gate of the Mists and climbed Nelion to descend by the normal route. We reached Top Hut at 18.30 and were back at Two Tarn to be congratulated by Michael at 20.30. He had watched our entire ascent from the Hut. It had been a challenging climb with an ideal companion. We had worked

The West Face. The two hanging glaciers on the right in shadow

well as a team, confident in each other's skill and we were destined to have other fine adventures together.

The following year two Austrians arrived at the clubhouse and announced an ambitious climbing plan on the mountain. They were displayed in the local press where it was stated that they were to put new routes up both Mount Kenya and Mount Kilimanjaro; they climbed neither and left quietly.

In contrast some two weeks later, two Germans arrived. Quiet and unassuming, they approached me and learned what knowledge they could about Mount Kenya. Walter Welsch from the Bayerland Section of the Deutschen Alpenverein was accompanied by Leo Hernkarek of the Oberland Section.

Right: Looking down the Heim glacier in the moonlight - R Baillie climbing

Below left: B Cliff on the Forel Glacier

Below right: R Baillie at the top of the Forel Glacier

Here were two mountaineers with vast experiences of Alpine climbing. "Which are the best climbs?" they asked. We went through the Guide Book together and they asked for details of all the routes. They were interested in the West Face. They left for the mountain two days later and twelve days after I joined them for a weekend. At Top Hut they told me what they had done. Their first climb was the third ascent of the Northey Glacier, a route Peter Campbell and I had done the previous month and they bivouacked on the summit. Three days later they did the West Face, again making a bivouac on the summit and descending the normal route. This was swiftly followed by an ascent of the West Ridge with again a high bivouac.

To us living in Kenya, and particularly those who had experienced a bitterly cold bivouac on the main peak it had always seemed best to have a very early start on the serious routes to Batian in order to complete the climb in a day and be off the peak by nightfall. There were numerous fatal accidents to the late parties attempting to descend the tricky loose normal southeast face route of Nelion. The two highly successful Germans had a different approach. In their climbing on Mount Kenya they had set out with a bivouac in mind, and hence they were in no hurry. They could enjoy the route to the full without a constant eye on the time, and to see the dawn from the summit of Batian must be an additional reward. They had a bivouac on the summit after climbing the Northey (third ascent), the West Face (fourth ascent) and the West Ridge. They told me of their adventures when I joined them for a weekend at Top Hut. I listened intently and could hardly believe their incredible success. Nothing seemed to deter these two highly experienced Alpine climbers and their approach seemed so much better then ours as Kenya residents.

Thompson's Flake

It was then that Leo suddenly announced he thought, "Thompson's Flake would go!" but it was described in the first edition of the Guide Book as a "decaying pinnacle of rotten rock" which nobody had been "crazy enough to ascend." I had walked past it a number of times and like everyone else who had done so was entirely in agreement with the Guide Book. Indeed it looked as if it would eventually fall over onto the Lewis Glacier.

Sitting with Leo and Walter at Top Hut and looking at the Flake across the Lewis Glacier they persuaded me to join them for an attempt and we ambled across the glacier but anticipating retreat I took the skis with me. We climbed to the col between the Flake and Thompson's Point and from here the Flake looked completely different. A broad couloir ran up to the shoulder about half-way up but Leo felt that a traverse left was a better line followed by an awkward corner and an overhang. He made short work of it and called for Walter to lead the second pitch, a further rising traverse and a corner from where he moved out of sight. Then he called me up. "One more pitch and this one is yours," he said. A short crack and an arête and I was on the precarious summit. Only room for two men so Leo joined me with Walter a little lower down. Leo had been correct and it proved to be an excellent climb. It started to snow and soon after building a cairn with the plentiful loose rocks, we put in a piton and abseiled with two hundred and forty feet of rope down the south side.

In the mist we walked back to Top Hut and I carried the skis. When the mist cleared we saw that the snow at the foot of the Flake was stained with debris we had

Thompson's Flake. The cairn built on the top after the first ascent can just be seen

knocked off during our climb. There are not quite so many loose rocks on it now! Whilst with them I told them of the virgin pillar of northeast Nelion. "No, we will not go on it," they said. "That is your route, Barry." They then descended the mountain and after a brief visit with me to Lukenya they left for Kilimanjaro where they made the first ascent of the Kersten Glacier in 2½ days. Some time later I read that Walter Welsch's party had made the first ascent of the Moose's Tooth in Alaska, an ascent upon which numerous international climbers had had their eye.

Equatorial Winter Sports

The Lewis Glacier on Mount Kenya is long and at a relatively

East face of Nelion with cloud in front – Thompson's Flake can be seen silhouetted beneath the cloud

gentle angle. It had occurred to me on numerous occasions that it would be quite possible to ski on it. With this in mind, on my first leave period back in England, I bought an old pair of skis with ancient bindings and took them back with me to East Africa. At the airport check-in point for the flight back the skis caused some hilarity, as they also did with the African customs officer on arrival at Nairobi, who of course queried what they were. A battered pair of skis adorning the mountain club bar provided a second pair, and so equipped Peter Campbell, Annemarie Weber and myself climbed to the Lewis

Glacier to exhibit our skills! Somehow a professional cameraman, Tony Carr, joined the group, hoping no doubt to get a "scoop" for the East African Standard.

At about 16,000 feet above sea level, climbing up and down the glacier was fatiguing and he got plenty of pictures of fallen skiers, in most unbecoming poses. It did, however, get me extremely fit and acclimatised, and once we had finished, Peter Campbell and I left the group to traverse round to the north side of the mountain to make the second ascent of the Northey Glacier route, climbed two years previously by Adams and Chambers as a Grade V ice route.

Glacier Flying

Apart from skiing on the Lewis Glacier on Mount Kenya it occurred to me that it might well be feasible to land an aircraft on it. On the numerous mountain rescues I had been involved in, getting the injured person lower down to an acceptable altitude for a helicopter to land and take off had always been an arduous task. Indeed Tony Levy had to be carried down to Klarwill's Hut (where his body lies to this day) and Kisoi Munyao, after the flag raising had to run down to that altitude to be lifted off by helicopter and flown down to the stadium for his presentation to the new President Jomo Kenyatta on Kenya becoming independent.

I had discussed the problems of rescue on the mountain with the Austrians after our east face climb and Wastl Mariner in particular, as a very experienced rescue team member in the

Austrian Alps recommended that the Mountain Club of Kenya should purchase a winch he had designed enabling an injured climber to be raised or lowered on a steel cable over a thousand feet long. (Such a winch was used to lower Alfred Hellepart in 1957 to the injured Italian climber Claudio Corti on the Eigerwand a thousand feet below. He attached Corti to his back and the two were then winched to the summit thus effecting a very successful rescue.) Wastl considered Mount Kenya to be an easy mountain for rescue since it would involve only lowering with the winch suitably situated above. I passed his sentiments to the Mountain Club and I hope they now have such an important piece of equipment!

I became fixated with glacier technique with aircraft and I purchased two books to learn more: "Der Gletscherflieger" by the famous Hermann Geiger and "Le Pilotage en Montagne" by JF Chappel and R Merloz. It all sounded so fascinating that in 1974, whilst I was flying for Air Kenya in Mombasa, I corresponded with Air Glaciers, based in Sion, Switzerland and arranged to visit the company on my next leave to undergo instruction in glacier flying. Arriving there I was met by a delightful lady, Aline Robard-Lesaffre who informed me that she would be teaching me. She questioned me at some length about my mountain experience and skiing capability, particularly if I was able to "read snow" and if I could recognise crevasse possibility! Suitably clothed, in the event of having to descend the mountain on foot, we took off from Sion airport in a Piper Cub equipped with skis on the wheels. She ably demonstrated how to assess the snow and how to select

Learning glacier flying in Switzerland

a suitable landing and take-off site whilst still airborne. In the course of ten days we did twenty-seven landings and take-offs on three different glaciers and under varying snow conditions. She awarded me an endorsement to my flying licence for glacier operation. Whilst there I made enquiries about the

63

purchase of skis for a Piper PA18 (Cub) and returned to Kenya where sadly my proposition for operating on the Lewis Glacier on Mount Kenya was not received too well by the Civil Aviation Department. I regret to this day that I did not pursue further and make the first landing on the mountain with a fixed wing aircraft.

It was a fascinating experience to learn the techniques with the aeroplane but the highlight of my visit was a meeting with Ramond Lambert, the Swiss climber from the Swiss Everest expedition one year before the successful British expedition with Edmund Hillary. Lambert, partnered by Tenzing almost climbed the mountain and they were the first to reach the south summit. I was introduced to him as he was climbing out of the swimming pool at Sion airport and he said, "Look, my footprints are like the abominable snowman in the Himalayas!" (his toes had been amputated after frostbite). After the expedition he had qualified as a glacier pilot and was operating a Pilatus Porter on skis for Air Glaciers. Although never having climbed on Mount Kenya, he considered that landing on the Lewis Glacier would be an interesting and worthwhile project and very useful for mountain rescue. I hope someone will take up the challenge and I am only sorry that I will not now have the opportunity.

Chapter 3

Nelion's northeast pillar and east face

The north face of Mt Kenya showing the twin peaks - Nelion left and Batian right. The north-east pillar of Nelion route starts on the Krapf glacier just above the shadow and takes a crack to the right of the grey pillar mid-route. Then under the overhang to the left at the top (where the catwalk is.)
Photo: E Schneider

The Pillar

Another year elapsed before I was able to get on the mountain again and this time I was anxious to attempt the northeast pillar of Nelion. Dennis Rutowitz and I approached the mountain by the northern Sirimon route in order that we could get a good view of the north face. It looked dry and relatively free of snow and ice. We decided to make our camp on the Krapf Glacier col immediately below the foot of the northeast pillar of Nelion and there we pitched two small mountain tents.

One of the tents in our camp on the Krapf col

First we made the second ascent of the French Piton Wall and bivouacked in a corner so that we might see the upper part of the Pillar in the first light of day, hoping that the sun would cast shadows of a likely traverse line across the great orange overhanging pillars of rock at the very top of the pillar. The French Piton Wall first ascent had been ten years previously and doubt had often been expressed that they had climbed to the summit of the mountain. Just above the corner where we bivouacked we found a cache of pitons and gear together with the C.A.F. (Club Alpin Français) flag suggesting that this was probably the French high point. They had

*Near the start of the northeast pillar of Nelion. Krapf glacier in the
background*

certainly climbed the most serious part of the route, however,
and the remaining section would have been merely
scrambling over easy loose rocks.

The time had come for action. Nervous, full of anticipation
and in the cold of dawn, Dennis and I stood at the foot of the
three hundred foot wall which faces east and abuts onto the
Krapf Glacier. The packs were heavy with food for two days
and full bivouac equipment with about thirty pitons and etriers.
We knew the line we had to take. It had seemed the only one
and it was now well imprinted on our minds. It was a relief to
feel the hard rock and to be at grips and completely absorbed
in the problem. Whatever was going on down at the foot of

the mountain was not our concern. Here was the problem, to get up this great mass of rock and nothing else mattered.

Beneath the pillar, at its extreme right hand edge a crack seemed to give the easiest line. We started at a point some thirty feet to the left of the crack and traversed into it at about eighty feet. There was an awkward mantelshelf move into the crack itself, where to our surprise we found it was the perfect width for "chimneying". We had to sack-haul for three pitches until the crack narrowed and was eventually sealed by a number of large unsafe blocks. We broke again onto the left wall and after a steep pitch gained the arête. The crack had taken us four hours. Without resting we tackled the Ramp and traversed across the face to the foot of the Grey Pillar, the most prominent feature of the face. Sitting in a niche as Dennis came up, my eyes wandered over this huge wall of rock. I remembered Rusty's letter; "Can you send me a picture of that great pillar on Nelion's north? It should go as a layback in the corner." What? ... five hundred feet of it at 16,000!!

From our French Piton Wall climb we had seen that the pillar was broken by two cracks on its northern aspect, so we traversed right until we could see the first crack. It looked possible. The first section was easy enough, but soon steepened and we came to grips with an overhanging little nose, which led to a recess at the foot of the last long pitch of the crack. After a few abortive attempts and not knowing what lay beyond, we decided to bivouac in the recess at the foot. A lump of ice in the corner provided us with a water supply and while dusk fell we sat and drank hot soup. The cold gradually crept in and huddled together we sat and shivered for the rest of the night.

Our first bivouac

As soon as dawn came we realised our mistake. Our bivouac site faced northwest and did not get the morning sun to warm us. No wonder there was a patch of ice! Slowly we began to get warm as we climbed awkwardly to our stance below the steep crack. It was long, about one hundred and twenty feet to the shoulder of the pillar and it took us three hours to climb. Here we rested and brewed some tea. The day was perfect and while we sat we picked out Ololokwe, the big rock mountain in the Northern Frontier District and way over to the northeast the Nyambeni Hills where I had planted tea and lived for a year and from where I had seen this very face of the mountain every day.

Sitting on top of the pillar we surveyed the great towering orange buttresses of rock above us. The line we had picked from the French Piton Wall now looked impossible and the only way seemed to be to climb up diagonally right, to what appeared to be a traverse line running just under the overhangs. We climbed broken slabs to reach the traverse line

71

Dennis on the second day. Our two tents can be seen on the Krapf col 1,200 feet below

beneath the wall of overhangs with occasional showers of ice coming from the top, off the summit ice slope. It was here that we found two hundred and fifty feet of a tangled coil of new nylon rope which the pilot had tried to drop on Nelion for Geoff Newham's rescue when he broke a leg just below the summit ten months previously. We coiled it and left it there for our descent. It might be useful on the way down, we thought. The traverse was quite easy to start with as we threaded our way round great boulders and blocks of ice. It soon gave way to harder climbing and before long we were confronted by a huge very steep, hold-less grey slab of rock. Our way was blocked but we could see our line continuing after the slab; it had to be crossed. It appeared that the only way over would be to tension traverse across on the rope with the aid of a high peg in the crack in which we stood. (To surmount a featureless passage across a rock wall, such as we were now faced with, a tension traverse can be arranged, always providing a high piton can be placed alongside and higher than the blank wall to be surmounted. By then leaning away from the anchor point and keeping tension on the rope and using friction with the feet, a lateral movement can be made in a pendulum action, enabling passage across the blank wall. Perhaps the most well known tension traverse was done my Andreas Hinterstoisser to gain access to the first ice field on an early attempt of the Eiger north face in 1936; now, of course known as the famous Hinterstoisser Traverse.) Dusk started to fall as we retreated down the traverse line to a small niche beneath the overhang where we spent our second bivouac, a wonderful airy perch, facing due east where we would

Dennis at the summit after 2½ days climbing

get the early morning sun.

In the morning we ate our last food before returning to the slab, which we named the Catwalk, where Dennis climbed the crack to put the tension peg in. He had an especially wide American piton which was ideal for the crack and after hammering it in he came down the rope with a huge grin across his face, assuring me that it gave an excellent anchor point for the tension traverse! Since the peg was not really high enough for the distance across the slab, the last few moves had to be made on friction holds. We tried three times before it yielded and it was a nasty feeling letting go of the tension rope. An awkward chimney followed then there was a broken gully. In our anxiety to reach the summit we discarded the rope, only to find that the mountain had not yet finished with us and we had to return to retrieve the rope for an awkward little pitch above. Over this the snowfield led to the ridge between Nelion and the Gate of the Mists. On familiar ground now we clambered to the summit.

A cold wind was blowing as mist swirled through the Gate, obliterating Batian as we started the long descent down our route. The Catwalk presented a real problem. Dennis thought we could "pendulum" across, but poised over that void we didn't feel like swinging. Eventually we cautiously abseiled diagonally across to below the ice curtain where we retrieved our bivouac gear and hurried on. Halfway down dusk started to fall and by the time we got to the arête it was pitch dark: only three hundred feet to go to the glacier and we felt very tempted to continue in the dark. Tired as we were and anxious to crawl into those beloved sleeping bags, prudence dictated that we should wait for the moon. When the moon rose four hours later and wracked with cold, we did two abseils down the face before the rope jammed, so we left it where it was and used the nylon rope we had found to get to the glacier, a further one hundred and twenty feet down. At 22.00 we trudged up to the col and the tents and blessed warmth and sleep. We had been away for sixty-four hours. It had been a tremendous climb.

The East Face

After the north-east pillar Dennis and I wandered over to Top Hut to do some skiing. To our surprise a great reception await-ed us. We found a party of Austrians there

Top Hut, Mt Kenya

under the leadership of Erwin Schneider who had come out from Innsbruck with the intention of doing what they called the two remaining climbs on Mount Kenya – the northeast pillar of Nelion and the East Face of Nelion. The previous day, whilst planning their climb, they had seen Dennis and me near the top. They were, of course, very disappointed and thought, "the bloody French have beaten us to it" (their words!). Being mountaineers they congratulated us heartily and asked that

Meeting with Austrians, 1963, Top Hut.
H Klier (seated, spectacles); Rutovitz (hatless); Wastl Mariner (hand over eyes); B Cliff (bearded); S Aeberli (white hat); C Brown (seated next to Klier)

The Austrians examining and borrowing our gear
(photo: E Schneider)

we might stand down and allow them first "go" at the East Face. Heinrich Klier and Siegfried Aeberli then accompanied Dennis and I back to our tents in the Knapf Col where we lent them our pitons, wooden wedges and etriers. (Whilst in Nairobi we had anticipated that we would be confronted by various sized cracks on the north east pillar of Nelion. We therefore made a number of wooden wedges of different sizes to jam into cracks

76

for belay points – the modern cam devices not then available). They set out on the following day to recce the route.

Dennis and I were spellbound watching them climb with speed over difficult unknown rock. Here were two climbers, fresh from the Alps worth watching but in a few hours snow started to fall and we lost sight of them in the mist. In two hours, however, they were back down the face and back at our camp drinking tea with us. They now knew about half the face and decided to try and get through in one day and not take bivouac gear. They wanted to descend by our northeast pillar route after climbing the east face and they suggested that Dennis and I should climb the east face with them as two ropes of two. Dennis declined as he did not feel fully recovered from our route, but they still wanted me to join them in a rope of three, which I readily accepted.

At 06.30 we assembled at the foot of the face and Heinrich led off. First two very nice pitches and then the third and hardest of all which Heinrich called, "The Inverted Staircase". This was Grade VI climbing and we did not get a stance for three hundred feet. We reached the "Raven's Nest" (Heinrich again) where we had a snack. Poised on this massive wall of rock we could see Dennis at the camp watching through binoculars and on Thompson's Point, Erwin and his fellow Austrians watching our progress and emitting the odd yodel. We pressed on, all hard vertical climbing, using a piton here and there for protection. It was my task, as third man, to take out the gear and carry it. We reached a shallow gully

Nelion – east face (photo: E. Schneider)

and climbed towards the final wall. Heinrich told Siegfried and I to watch out as he pushed a loose boulder he had come across down the wall. We heard it land on the glacier what seemed minutes later. At the final wall we came across the "Black Crack" (Heinrich again) soaring up to the summit. Still in the lead, he reached a point at which the angle appeared to ease but he required one of our wooden wedges to get fifteen feet further and we had none left. He offered me the lead and I climbed up to him to take a look. I reached

78

Key:
IS: Inverted
Staircase

RN: Raven's Nest

F: Funnel

BC: Black Crack

HC: Hourglass
Crack

SC: Sinister Crack

East face route (left) and part of northeast pillar route (photo: E. Schneider).

the same conclusion, a wedge was required, so we retreated and joined by Siegfried traversed off to the right across a very airy ledge.

Heinrich round the corner, suddenly shouted, "There are footsteps here in the snow!" – but there couldn't be! Had someone been here before us? Slowly I realised we were joining the gully out of which Dennis and I had come two days before. We unroped and hurried to the summit; it was

79

Above left: H Klier on East Face
Above right: S Aeberli on East Face
Left: B Cliff on East Face
Bottom: H Klier in the Black Crack

17.00. Way below we could see Erwin's red anorak at Top Hut and over on Firmin's Tower we could see Wastl Mariner and Theo Plattner (from the Austrian team) who were descending the north face route they had climbed to Batian. Heinrich gave a rich yodel which echoed round the mountain.

Then the descent. All the sling points were fixed from the descent with Dennis two days previously and we quickly reached a point near the arête. As with Dennis, here darkness fell and once again we waited for the moon. Both Heinrich and Siegfried were very impressed by the length of the route for it seemed we would never reach the glacier. We heard a shout from Dennis who had brought our ice axes to the foot of the climb. At midnight we staggered up to the camp where Dennis had a hot meal ready for us. Suitably refreshed, Heinrich and Siegfried left for Top Hut while I crawled into my sleeping bag. It had been a great day and I felt very privileged to have been with real mountain men and to have shared such a fine climb – the first Grade VI on the mountain.

Watching my attempts at skiing on the Lewis Glacier later, accompanied by a rich yodel every time I fell, the Austrians invited me to Austria "to learn to ski properly the Austrian way." After leaving Kenya I did go to Austria and worked for Heinrich on his ski lift on the Glungetzer in the winter season, climbing and skiing with these fine men again.

Chapter 4

Kenya Independence

Kenya was to become independent on December 12th, 1963, which would result in termination of my employment with the U.K. Government. In the Government, a Director of the Independence Celebrations was appointed and he was instructed to "investigate the possibility of carrying a torch to the peak of Mount Kenya and raising the new National Flag there at midnight on the eve of Independence"; accordingly he contacted the Mountain Club. Those of us who knew the mountain realised that this timing was in the short rains period when there would be poor weather on the mountain and a strong possibility of heavy snowfall. The rains normally end before mid-December, and we were aware that Eric Shipton with his partner Russell had made a successful ascent of Nelion and Batian on December 17th, 1929, encountering "much ice".

The then President of the Mountain Club, Robert Chambers, handled the request to the Club and whilst immediately discounting the torch idea felt that "no-one could take exception to the idea of raising a National Flag on the summit, but was it right to expose a climbing party to a place of publicity and a psychological build-up that might press them into unjustifiable risks?" His feelings were not universally accepted and one eminent climber expressed his distaste at putting a flag on any mountain, let alone a beautiful high one that had such reverence amongst many of us. Myself I had similar sentiments, but the party built up quickly and I was invited. On learning that those selected would be automatically granted leave from their various employment positions and that funds would be provided to purchase new climbing gear, my sentiments easily mellowed and when, to my delight, I was put in charge of ordering all the new equipment, I hastily accepted. I ordered bivouac sacs, duvets, pied d'elephant, ice screws, head torches and 1,200 ft of rope from France, and imagined at last, comfortable bivouacs in luxury on that very cold mountain.

The party expanded quickly in number with many "hangers-on". There were to be broadcasts from the actual climb, a film was to be made and a helicopter would be made available to fly Kisoi Munyao (the Kamba African selected to be with the summit party) off the lower slopes of the mountain after the flag had been raised to the Nairobi Stadium where he would be presented to the new President (Jomo Kenyatta) and Prince Philip. Others were given crash courses on ciné photography, radio operation and a local car dealer offered the use of two Austin Gypsy 4-wheel drive vehicles for test on the rough track up the mountain. The President of the Mountain Club, Robert Chambers, by profession an administrative officer in the Colonial Service was in his hey-day and described it all later as "hectic and tremendous fun."

Living "up country" I missed all this but was called down to Nairobi to handle an altercation with Customs officials that had developed when the new climbing equipment arrived at the airport. Anticipating that the mountains would be well covered with snow I suggested to the President that the south face route (a snow and ice route) would be the best line to take to the summit, but he favoured the normal route up the southeast ridge of Nelion. To try to assess the two routes he and I were flown by the Police Air Wing around the mountain on 23rd November. We were able to see that the southeast ridge was under snow and ice and that there was a good snow covering on the proposed south face route. Later on that same day, Kisoi Munyao, John Hull, the President and I walked up the mountain to take a closer look. On the following day, from Two Tarn Hut, we climbed the first few pitches of the south face to find poor soft snow conditions but there was nothing to suggest that the route would be unduly difficult. On the day after, from Top Hut, we had a look at the normal southeast ridge route as it was snowing and it took us some time to climb the first few pitches. Preference was then voiced for the south face route and with this decision made we descended to Nairobi to await the "cavalcade" departure of the main group from the Mountain Club premises on 2nd December.

It was raining at Naro Moru and the track up the mountain was thick with mud and it was not long before I man-aged to get one of the loaned Austin Gypsies stuck

Austin Gypsy stuck in mud on Mt Kenya track, with Kisoi Munyao

85

down a 10-foot ravine. It was ignominiously winched out by John Hull's indefatigable Land Rover and eventually the whole group assembled at the Meteorological Station to begin the walk up the track to the peaks.

At the head of the Teleki valley a camp site was selected but with incessant rain and sleet it quickly became a quagmire with the President and myself coming under severe criticism for the "pathetic site". For most of our time there the weather and the camp site displayed a wilful perversity.

John Hull knee deep in snow on the south face and carrying 300ft of rope to fix higher up for the main party

John Hull and myself were selected to be the lead climbers of the summit party of six and carrying three hundred feet of rope to fix higher up the mountain, John and I left camp at 03.00 on 9th December with a proposed bivouac on the summit ready for raising the flag at midnight on the 11th. We had a hard time of it and at times were waist deep in soft snow, forging our way up the snow of the Darwin glacier. We were across the traverse by dawn and by 08.00 were two pitches up the snowfields, carefully belaying on the few outcrops of rock we found. The going was slow and very tiring for whoever was in the lead. My right foot became frozen and several times I removed the boot to massage my big toe. John also started to suffer with cold feet. I turned to John and suggested that flag or no flag, we should descend. However, where we were poised, the four following climbers caught up with us and at 10.30 we roped as a six with Dennis in the lead.

At midday we reached the rock at the top of the snowfield and at that moment, with a long roar, the surface of the Diamond glacier to our left avalanched and slid away. It had been our intention to traverse *across* it to the summit of Batian! We were badly placed and now faced with a five hundred foot traverse to the east across the foot of Mackinder's Gendarme where we could join and descend the southeast ridge route. Dennis led the traverse, the last pitch involving 120 feet of rope where there was a long discussion on the number of people on one rope and the precarious situation we had become involved in, all for the sake of the flag, with one member announcing that "the flag must go up!"

By 17.00 we had all reached the base of Mackinder's Gendarme, and whilst we had been in mist, the route of descent below had received some sun and the rocks were warm and dry. We descended safely and reached camp at 20.30. Here the doctor examined my foot and reported that it was in a serious condition with no question of me climbing again. John was also given the same diagnosis for his feet. The decision was then made to abandon the south face route in favour of the normal southeast ridge route and with a depleted party, those still capable of climbing left for Top Hut. They were successful in reaching the subsidiary peak Nelion and duly raised the flag there at midnight. Kisoi was in the summit party and after descending lower was able to be flown by helicopter to the presentation to Jomo Kenyatta at the Nairobi Stadium. John and I staggered off the mountain in heavy rain and spent the night sheltering under his Land Rover. Both of us had frostbite and we were incapacitated for a considerable time.

Chapter 5

Mount Kilimanjaro to Mount Kenya in under 24 hours (1964)

Our plans for the big routes on Mount Kenya had been washed out. In January, usually a month of good weather, there had been continuous rain and snow as we sat out the bad weather at Top Hut. Rusty Baillie had joined me in Kenya at the beginning of January and we had still not done a climb together. We were getting frustrated. The first time we had met had been on Mount Kenya in 1961 when we had made the 3rd ascent of the great West Face and we had subsequently climbed together on Table Mountain in Cape Town, South Africa, before Rusty had moved to Scotland to accept guiding and instructing employment in Glencoe with Hamish MacInnes.

Fresh from a fine ascent of the Eigerwand in Switzerland with Dougal Haston he was fit and eager for a good adventure. His only comment on the Eiger was, "The big black wall was fun." At Top Hut on Mount Kenya we wondered if we could climb Kilimanjaro (19,340 feet), then race to Mount Kenya 286 miles away and climb the highest peak, Batian

R Baillie (left) and B Cliff climbing Atlantic Crack on Table Mountain (photo: M Mamacos)

91

(17,085 feet) all within twenty-four hours. It was an idea first mentioned to me at the Mountain Club of Kenya in Nairobi some months previously and I had initially discarded it. What was needed, we wondered? Intimate knowledge of both mountains, supreme fitness – and a very fast car. True we had both done the climb to Batian many times but neither of us had been on Kilimanjaro. We did have a fast car though (my Jaguar XK150). We reckoned that the climb to Batian should be done early morning and the walking/running part in darkness, so we planned to climb Kilimanjaro first, leaving the summit at midday and to be on Mount Kenya's summit twenty-four hours later by midday on the second day.

Kilimanjaro by the normal tourist route does not involve any actual rock or ice climbing but it is very high and many people are defeated by altitude. Most people take four or five days to get up and down it. The normal route on Mount Kenya, however, is a Grade IV rock climb, first pioneered by Eric Shipton and takes normal parties four to five hours from Top Hut to the summit of Nelion, the lower of the twin peaks. Then the Gate of the Mists must be crossed to Batian, the higher peak. The crossing normally takes about 1½ hours, there is only 300 feet of it, but it is high, often iced up and very exposed. As we talked it all seemed feasible and we even thought of having a rest and sleep at Top Hut on Mount Kenya before tackling the peak!

As the bad weather continued we descended Mount Kenya to Naro Moru where we discussed our proposed venture with

Game Warden, Bill York. It was good to sense his enthusiasm and he promised to wait at the foot of Mount Kenya at Naro Moru at midnight after we had climbed Kilimanjaro. We then headed off to Sultan Hamud, a village on the north side of Kilimanjaro. Just before we got there, testing our nerve at high

The Jaguar XK150 on the murram road after Sultan Hamud

speed in the Jaguar, we had a disaster on a sharp rock. The fuel tank was cracked but the local mechanic in Sultan Hamud reckoned he could remove it, solder and replace it and then fill it with fuel. "It's important," I remember telling him, "that it must be ready by 7pm tomorrow because we're racing." Then we got a lift to Loitokitok and spoke with the warden of the Outward Bound school. "I'll drive you to your Jag at Sultan Hamud after you've done Kili," he said. "Take one of my instructors with you – Ken Ledward: he has the record up and down Kili and he'll pace you." So Ken, Rusty and I walked up to Third Cave at 12,300 feet that evening. Our day had been exhausting and we had such a comfortable bivouac that we overslept! Already behind schedule, it seemed impossible to get to the summit of Kilimanjaro, 7,000 feet above us by

*Above: Our comfortable bivouac before
climbing to Kilimanjaro summit
Left: B Cliff on the summit of Mt
Kilimanjaro at 14.00 (photo: R Baillie)*

midday and, sure enough it was impossible and at 12.00 we were still struggling up that awful scree. We left Ken there and continued, staggering round the rim to the summit, which we reached at 14.00. In deep snow those last few feet were agony and we were both so tired that it seemed very unlikely that we would ever get to Mount Kenya. After a brief pause for photographs the race was on.

R Baillie (left) and B Cliff running down from the summit of Kilimanjaro

First we had to travel halfway round the summit crater rim following our knee-deep tracks in the snow. After our arduous ascent it was easy going and before long we were overlooking the great scree slope. We glissaded down the snow and bounded down the scree to Ken. Without a pause we carried on, Ken in the lead and setting a cracking pace. It was a relief to be going down and it took 1½ hours to do that 7,000 feet back to Third Cave, that 7,000 feet which had taken us seven hours to climb! We then paused and changed into light running shoes and jogged on. Way down below we could see Loitokitok where the Warden would be waiting for us,

95

but before that we had to get through the forest. This worried us no end, for it would be getting dusk, the time when the big game starts to move. What would we do if we ran into a herd of elephant? Elephant, in spite of their great size, move very quietly in the forest and it would be very easy to suddenly find ourselves in the midst of a herd. Indeed, a friend of mine had been hurled against a tree and killed by an elephant when he inadvertently walked between mother and calf in the forest. Ken consoled us; he hadn't seen many elephant on that side of the mountain.

As we got to the lower altitude we began to feel better and our hopes built up. Soon the moorland gave way to trees

and before long we entered the forest. We trotted silently on. Anxious to be out of the forest by nightfall the pace quickened, mainly through fear I think and before long we emerged from the forest edge and trotted through some African farms down to the village. It was 19.00 when we reached the Outward Bound school where Derek Pritchard awaited us with his

B Cliff running through the forest

96

Land Rover. After a quick drink and thanks to Ken for accompanying us we hurtled away with Derek at the wheel. We had planned to sleep on the 70 mile journey to Sultan Hamud, but as we dodged giraffe, warthog and various other animals, sleep was impossible. With a howl of tyres we reached Sultan Hamud where we had left the Jaguar. There was the Jag all ready with the mechanic grinning broadly at our urgency. I tipped him another 100 shillings and with a hurried thanks to Derek off we tore into the night with 100mph bursts on the dusty road. We drove into the night, drinking pint after pint of liquid, for we were very dehydrated after running down Kilimanjaro and at the same time driving as fast as the road would allow (not tarmac in those days).

We by-passed Nairobi and headed north, a familiar road to me and now on tarmac we speeded on. The sky was dark and we worried about the weather on "The Mountain" – if we got bad weather on the normal route it would take much longer to climb than we anticipated. At 23.30 we turned into Naro Moru and sure enough there was Bill with hot drinks ready for us. We had averaged 86mph on the leg from Sultan Hamud and we felt well satisfied. We were running ahead of schedule so we rested for ten minutes with the drinks whilst Bill got his Land Rover ready for the road up the mountain. We found the track in terrible condition following the recent rains and there were great gullies running down the middle of the road. Bill expertly wrestled with the wheel and with magnificent handling got us to the Meteorological Station clearing at 9,000 feet in record time. At 02.00 we started to walk again, this time with Bill in the lead and setting the pace.

Our legs were stiff and we had foot blisters as we started that long walk up to Mount Kenya's Top Hut, a distance of about ten miles and a rising height of 6,000 feet. We trudged up after Bill until eventually we broke out of the forest and came to the moorlands. The track immediately after the forest is referred to by many climbers as the "vertical bog", and it fits its name.

Knee deep in mud we trudged on, hardly caring where we put our feet. Just as our spirits were getting to a really low ebb, Bill came out with his trump card – a flask containing a mixture of brandy and home-brewed wine. It did the trick and the pace quickened. At Klarwill's Hut we stopped as dawn approached and I felt so hungry that I ate an old sandwich we found there. I was immediately sick and Rusty reprimanded me for eating it. After the moorlands we came to the steep scree which leads up to Top Hut and whilst we were on this the brilliant African dawn we wanted turned into a grey overcast ominous sky. We hurried on to Top Hut where Tom Phillips awaited us with a hot drink. It was 07.00.

After a brief rest we changed into climbing gear, picked up the rope and slings and trudged across the Lewis Glacier to the start of the route. What a relief it was to be on rock and we both got a second life. Climbing solo we quickly reached Mackinder's Gendarme and roped for Eric Shipton's Rickety Crack. After one hour and forty minutes of ascent we stood on the summit of Nelion at 10.30 where we rested briefly as we got the ice axe out. The Gate of the Mists was heavily

*R Baillie coiling our rope on the summit of Batian (Mt Kenya) 21 hours
and 40 minutes after leaving the summit of Kilimanjaro (photo B Cliff)*

corniced and all ice. We cautiously cut into it and climbed out
of the other side onto the summit rocks of Batian and after a
couple of rope pitches, we climbed to the summit. It was 11.30,
twenty-one hours and forty minutes since leaving the summit
of Kilimanjaro, just visible to us above cloud over two hundred
miles away.

At Top Hut down below we could see Bill, just arriving, and
later verifying that he had seen us on the summit. As we rested
snow started to fall. We made our descent carefully down to
Top Hut. Bill had a meal ready for us there, but we couldn't
eat. All we wanted was a hot bath and sleep. The weather was
deteriorating rapidly so we decided to get off the mountain
as soon as we could. We started the long walk down with Bill.

By the time we got to the "vertical bog" it was dark again. Supporting each other and covered in mud we had another nightmare journey across it, down to Bill's Land Rover. We reached Bill's farm at 01.00 where I took my hot bath. By the time I had finished Rusty, still covered in mud, was already asleep. We had been on the move for forty-two hours!

Later next day I went to Naro Moru to collect the Jag. I looked underneath to see what the repair was like. There it was: a piece of soap! The mechanic had not even bothered to remove the tank, let alone solder it! He had simply used an African trick of sealing a petrol leak. A piece of soap is moistened with water in the hands and kneaded into a suitable consistency. It is then simply pressed in the leak, where it will dry, stick and harden – enough for only a temporary repair. I looked for that mechanic for years afterwards!

Although at the time we were accused of seeking publicity there was in fact very little, but Rusty later published an article in the Scottish *Daily Express* in 1964. Twenty-one years later the Editor of *Climber and Rambler* magazine in England requested an article from me (*Climber and Rambler*, December 1985). The ascent of the two mountains within twenty-four hours has now remained unrepeated for forty-three years (2007).

In retrospect it was a great test of stamina and comradeship. We were near the limit of physical exhaustion, but we enjoyed every minute of it. It was great to have lived at such a pace.

An organisation named the "Rhino Ark Charitable Trust" attempted to stage a re-enactment of our event of what they called "The Great East African Mountain Charge" at the Millennium (2000), but administrative problems were encountered and it was eventually abandoned.

Sadly, Rusty and I never climbed together again. He returned to instructing in Scotland and eventually the U.S.A., with many other fine climbs. I tried to climb again after the aircraft accident in 1965, but the physical injury I suffered restricted me. I was unable to experience the same enjoyment in rock climbing and it only resulted in frustration at losing the strength and agility I had been blessed with. It was time to look for other adventures.

Times, Kili to Kenya

				Driver
3rd Cave	(12 300ft) 07.00	} 7.00 hours walking		
Kili Summit	(19 340ft) 14.00	} 4.30 hours running		
Outward bound Loitokitok	(3 000ft) 18.30	} 1.30 hours driving	Land Rover	Derek Pritchard
Sultan Hamud } 286 miles	(3 000ft) 20.00	} 3.30 hours driving	Jag XK150	Barry Cliff
Naro Moru	(5 500ft) 23.30	} 2.30 hours driving	Land Rover	Bill York
Met clearing	(9 000ft) 02.00	} 5.00 hours walking		
Top Hut	(15 500ft) 07.00	} 3.30 hours climbing		
Nelion	(16 700ft) 10.30	} 1.10 hours climbing		
Batian	(17 038ft) 11.40	} 4.20 hours		
Top Hut	(15 500ft) 16.00	} descending		
Met clearing	(9 000ft) 23.00	} 7.00 hours walking	Land Rover	Bill York
Bill's Farm (Nyeri)	(6 000ft) 03.00	2.00 hours driving		

42 hours overall
Summit to Summit 21 hours 40 minutes

Extract from Climber and Rambler, *December 1985*

Chapter 6

An epic with John Cleare
(Two Voices)

"Two Voices are there – one is of the Sea, One of the Mountains; each a mighty voice" (William Wordsworth, 1770-1850, writing of his 'Thoughts of a Briton on the Subjugation of Switzerland'). They both beckon a man. Some can hear both, some can hear only one, others cannot hear either, but to hear both at the same time can be dangerous.

"Swanage", they said, "that's the place to climb in England these days." I listened with some apprehension for after Kenya, small crags did not appeal any more. "Are you a strong swimmer?" they asked, "You should go and try the unclimbed buttress." John Cleare had taken part in many of the new climbs and in the summer of 1963 he and Rusty were the first to climb "traverse of the Gods at Swanage", named in recognition of Rusty's Eigerwand ascent only a few months previously. John gave more details of climbing at Swanage and we planned to go down there together on the following November weekend.

The only way down to the traverse was to abseil from a fence post at the top of the cliff, 200 feet of it and at the bottom you traverse to the foot of the crack. "What happens if we don't get up?" I cautiously asked. "We traverse off," said John, "for about half a mile, we might get our feet wet, though." It all sounded intriguing and I was duly tempted.

First we did one of the recognised climbs so that I would get used to the feel of the limestone rock. The outcome was that it was already well into the afternoon when we did our long abseil down towards the pounding sea beneath. We found the ledge and started our traverse to the unclimbed buttress. There was an eerie feeling down there, civilisation was only 200 feet above us but we felt cut off. Here was our problem of steep rock and sea and already it seemed urgent but John consoled me. "The traverse is easy," he said.

Soon we were engrossed. The sun was shining and we were warm and happy as we inched our way upwards. A channel peg followed by a couple of étrier moves up to a nasty overhang.

I think we both realised at the same time; it was getting dark. Let's try to get just a few feet more before we leave it for another day and begin the traverse back, we thought. The sun set into the sea and then the cold started. "Time to go," said John and we collected our gear and began the traverse.

It was easy to start with. Hopping from boulder to boulder we made rapid progress but when darkness really set in care was vital and soon movement became painfully slow. A cold wind started to blow and the sea became angry. We still had about a quarter of a mile to go and already it was a nasty scene. A hand traverse followed across a wall only a few feet above the sea. John led and I could only just make him out in the darkness. Suddenly there was a roar from the sea and a great wave broke over him. When the sea had receded he was still there alright and he hurried back with the awful news that he had lost his glasses. "You will have to lead," he said, "I can't see." The situation was bad; unknown rock with a sea anxious to prove its mighty strength. We roped now, not with the idea of holding each other if we fell but with the idea of pulling each other from the dreadful sea if it tried to snatch us again. The hand traverse went safely but the next few moves were tricky and it slowly became a very fight for life. It was not long before we had both been completely immersed in the sea and it was at this moment that the words of an old sailor friend of mine came back to me. "Never fight the sea," he had said, "use the sea and treat it as a friend but never fight it." We were in a situation now where we had to. It was impossible to bivouac where we were and in the dark we doubted we could scale the crag. Survival would be a question of swimming for it across the awful gulf we were now confronted with.

Slowly I slid into the water but with rucksack and boots on I doubted I could swim far. I remember standing on a boulder when a wave caught me and I then recall being somersaulted about three times before cracking my face on a lump of rock underwater. Then I felt a tug of the rope as John pulled me back. This was crazy and clearly the sea had won. We shut out its voice and listened to the other. We decided to use all of the tricks of our trade and try to climb the cliff in the darkness. We assembled all our pitons and gear on the rock we were standing on and faced the crag.

Suddenly there was a shout and a light shone down on us from the top. It was another climber who had seen us go down the cliff in the afternoon and he had been waiting for our return. Soon a rope came snaking down to us and we started the long business of climbing up it. My midnight we were safe at the top, but both shaking, partly from the cold but more from that feeling of having been at the very brink of life.

Later on in that month we picked a fine day with a calm sea and we returned and finished the unclimbed buttress just to show the sea that the fight was not over … but it was laughing at us as it played amongst the rocks below.

Chapter 7

Crocodile Encounter

As we sat under the Casuarina tree at Malindi and watched the surf of the Indian Ocean it had all seemed very feasible and we had talked of relaxing and sunbathing as the canoe drifted slowly down the river. We had even discussed making a film of all the game we anticipated seeing, but after the event we had a very different story to tell.

The idea had arisen after we had visited the Uaso Nyiro river earlier in the year. There, at Archer's Post the river had seemed slow and placid and it had appeared to be ideal for a canoe trip. A cursory glance at the map indicated that for fifty miles up river from Archer's Post it would be slow and meandering and its disappearance lower down into what was described as "The Lorian Swamp" sounded fascinating. Here was a part of Kenya virtually unexplored and the river had certainly never been navigated before.

Slowly the idea took shape and canoe plans were obtained. Constructing the craft out in the wilds of Kenya was in itself interesting work and there were many problems to be overcome but eventually we had an eighteen foot canoe, built of camphor wood and canvas covered, capable of carrying two men and equipment. It was launched on a nearby lake and named Casuarina after the tree we had sat under. It seemed easy to handle and slowly confidence grew. At the time we didn't imagine anything but success; after all, we had both courted danger many times in our mountaineering and we had no fear of a placid river! Shortly after the launching, however, my friend was unexpectedly sent back to England

Top: The canoe ready for the canvas
Above: First trial on Nairobi Dam, my dog "Ruff" the first passenger

and the problem of finding another partner presented itself. Maybe others realised the dangers. In any event nobody could be persuaded until some six months later when a fellow mountaineer was talked into it.

With the canoe on top of a Land Rover we went first to the small native village of Wamba and from there across bush

110

country to the river fifty miles up-stream from Archer's Post. Sure enough the river was slow and placid. Full of confidence we waved goodbye to the Land Rover driver and set about stowing our equipment into the canoe. We felt very much alone as we pushed off into mid-stream but a solitary Samburu tribesman raised his hand in farewell as the current out in the river slowly took over.

The first mile was just as we imagined and it all seemed too easy but on the next bend there, lying basking in the sun was a huge eighteen-foot yellow crocodile. It saw us immediately and slid silently into the water. Paddling furiously we expected it to surface alongside us but the river remained quiet and mysterious and we were left in doubt, but not for long. Round the next bend we saw another crocodile, dark green in colour

There were crocodiles of every size and colour. (Photo B Cliff)

and obviously of a different temperament to the first one. It swam fast on the surface to come and look at us. In desperation we thrashed at it with the paddles and it slowly submerged. Once again we paddled fast, expecting action at any minute. We got it all right when one of the paddles touched another crocodile lying on the bottom of the river. A thick powerful tail came up and thrashed between us, very nearly upsetting us. We evaded this one but soon realised that the whole river was infested with them. From then on we saw crocodile of every size and colour, each one reacted differently and they were completely unpredictable. Some swam up to look at us, others submerged whilst others just lay on the bank and watched our every movement. Clearly we were in a very dangerous situation and one which was almost out of our control. We were at the mercy of the crocodile and all they had to do was upset the canoe and we would be easy prey.

As if to aggravate the situation, the river at this point became fast-flowing and we shot down some small rapids, desperately trying to keep the canoe straight. Our problem was that we were unable to see the rapids from up-stream since we were so low in the water and we were on them before we could take evasive action. Once in a rapid, there was no going back and in this way we found ourselves shooting some very rough water. We were even plunged over a small waterfall and the river became so fast flowing that we were unable to reach the bank. Round the next bend we saw that the river narrowed and to our horror a fallen tree lay across it only inches above the water level. There was no time to take any action and we were forced into it. My friend in front held on to the tree and we became broadside on to the flow. With a tremendous crack the canoe folded and filled beneath us. Cameras, sleeping bags and most of our equipment floated away down-stream whilst we held on to the tree and tried to save the canoe. Any second we expected to be surrounded by crocodile but there was no time for fear. After a struggle, we managed to get the canoe to the bank but it was in a sorry state. We felt that it could be repaired but our paddles, the most important item had been washed down-stream. Carrying the damaged canoe between us we walked on the river bank alongside the river until we came to calmer water and there, stuck in mid-stream, were the paddles. There was no alternative but for one of us to wade in to get them. It was an ideal place for crocodile and as I waded in I thought I could sense movement. Suddenly there was a terrific thrashing sound and I turned to see a crocodile between me and the bank. I grabbed a paddle and turned to face it but it swam slowly away. With my heart in my mouth I regained the bank. Clearly we had tempted fate enough. The only solution was to abandon the remains of the canoe and walk out. With only an hour of daylight left that day we decided to sleep by the river and start walking the following day. To add to our troubles a rhino visited us towards dusk but it only wanted to drink and it soon thundered off into the bush.

Sleep was impossible for the whole bush seemed to come alive with activity. A herd of buffalo passed very close to us and we heard a lion roar and later an elephant scream. Thankful to be still alive at dawn, we started to walk along the river bank as soon as it was light enough.

It seemed best to follow the river down to Archer's Post estimated at about thirty miles but it was difficult walking and at the end of the day we had not done more than ten miles. Towards evening we came across three Samburu tribesmen who had been hunting in the area and we conversed in Swahili with them. They were horrified at our story and they invited us back to their *manyatta* to spend the night with them in safety.

After a further ten miles walk to their *manyatta* our troubles were virtually over and it was a great comfort to sit in their camp as night approached. On the following day we walked across country back to Wamba and civilisation. It had been a frightening experience from which we were lucky to escape with our lives and completely unscathed. What a hair-brained epic!

Chapter 8

Adventures in Aviation 1

Early Days

We were planning to spend some time on Mount Kenya and needed the help of porters to get our food and equipment up onto the mountain. Nanyuki town lies on the west side of the 17,500 ft mountain and its foot is virtually on the equator at 1,500 ft above sea level, and porters could be recruited there. Michael Robinson had recently learned to fly, so instead of the five hour return journey by road he made an afternoon flight there from Nairobi and organised our porters all in a couple of hours. This impressed me so much that I started taking flying lessons myself at Wilson Airport, and at forty-two flying hours, sixteen of which were logged as solo, I was requested to take the necessary flight test at Wilson Airport where the Mountain Club of Kenya also had its club house alongside the runway. They usually had a weekly meeting there every Tuesday evening so I arranged the test for late on a Tuesday afternoon in order to go later to their meeting.

I had taken flying lessons in a Piper Cub which has the two seats in tandem with the instructor at the dual controls and sitting in the seat behind the pupil. Very early on in the lessons I was taught the correct terminology for changing control from student to instructor is for the instructor to say, "I have control" and the pupil to always acknowledge by replying, "You have control". Similarly for the pupil wishing to relinquish the control and passing it to the instructor. In that way there should be no confusion who is flying the aeroplane!

The examiner, clearly ex-RAF, duly met me and we climbed into the Piper Cub with him in the rear seat. After two or three landings and circuits with me at the controls he asked me to climb the aeroplane to 3,000 feet above the airfield which I then did. Once we were in level flight he then asked me to do an "incipient spin". Well, I knew how to do a spin but what on earth was an "incipient spin"? Since I was on test I did not venture to ask, but simply thought I would demonstrate a normal spin. Accordingly I closed the throttle, lifted the nose to stall the aeroplane, gave it full right rudder and we were soon nose down and spinning clockwise down to earth. I held the aeroplane in this attitude awaiting further instructions. I sensed all was not well behind but casting all etiquette aside the examiner suddenly shouted, "For Christ's sake let go!" I took my feet off the rudder and he then applied throttle to gain level flight. The next instruction was to join the circuit and land the aeroplane. I duly obliged and taxied back to base. He then asked me, "What the hell do you think you're doing?" and informed me that I had failed the test. I then went to the Mountain Club to find two club members sitting outside with a beer on the terrace. They said I had missed a fine spectacle of an aeroplane out of control and very nearly spinning into the ground. I admitted that I was the culprit and had just failed the test. Some months later I took another test and managed to pass. Then I learned that an incipient spin is by putting the aeroplane into a stall, just getting into the symptoms of a spin but correcting before the spin occurs. Little wonder the initial examiner was terrified.

At the time I was living on the Mwea Plains and working on the rice irrigation scheme, sharing a house with Dutchman John Bol. He was to be my first passenger and wanted to film the take-off with his new 8mm cine camera. Sitting beside me in the dual-controlled aeroplane he started to film as I opened the throttle and we rolled down the runway. We were just about to become airborne when he stopped filming and stretched his legs out in the cramped cockpit. His right leg happened to touch the rudder bar and he gave the aeroplane full right rudder. Not at first realising what the problem was we became airborne in what was apparently a very impressive "crabbed" attitude, to be immediately asked by the Control Tower if all was well. After knocking his leg off the pedal we regained control but we had very nearly succeeded in writing the aeroplane off without leaving the ground!

Some time later I was fortunate enough to befriend Dr Michael Wood who had a small private aeroplane and was about to start the Flying Doctor Service. He periodically asked me to fly his aeroplane to pick up patients in remote places and I relished the experience of bush flying and using unprepared landing strips. With my limited flying experience and qualifications it was all done by VFR (Visual Flight Rules), and, as a Private Pilot, an acceptable qualification to fly his aircraft at that time (1963). One particular flight very nearly ended in disaster and was due entirely to my own fault. Whilst learning to fly it was made quite clear to me by the instructor that as a VFR pilot I should take great care not to go near to or into cloud until I had learned to fly "on instruments". The flight involved taking a veterinary officer and his lady assistant to Maralal on the northern frontier, a flight of about 1½ hours. In marginal weather we were given permission for a "special VFR" flight which really meant the conditions were such that the weather minima were really for IFR (Instrument Flight Rules) flights. We duly took off and headed north. At first we were able to climb to about 2,000 ft below cloud, but soon the cloud base became lower and in order to maintain the compass heading we had to descend to keep visual with the ground and out of cloud. We flew lower and lower and were very quickly at tree-top height! The cloud seemed to be only a thin layer, and in spite of all the instruction I had received I made the rash decision to climb through it. We entered cloud in a climbing attitude and within seconds I became completely disorientated. With no instrument flying experience at all, the instruments were soon spinning wildly as I fought for control. With the air speed indicator showing a rapid deceleration, the compass spinning and the artificial horizon at all angles I believe we must have soon been very nearly inverted. Indeed I was thrown upwards with such force that my knee bent the shaft of the starter key! Still fighting for control we fell out of the cloud. A shout of, "It's there!" from the front passenger showed us to be in a valley and surrounded by hills with their summits in cloud. With now visual reference I regained control and calculated a reciprocal heading on the compass to get out of the valley and return to Wilson Airport. Within half an hour, and very much chastened, we landed safely. I suggested to my passengers that we would wait for a weather improvement to take off again and to my amazement they agreed and we duly had an uneventful flight to Maralal. It had been a very lucky escape and I never ventured near cloud again until I had more qualifications and experience.

My next flight to Maralal on the northern frontier was some years later when Rusty Baillie was with me. We wanted to climb on Naibor Enkeju ("White Foot" in the Samburu language) – a fine rock mountain a few miles from Maralal. I chartered a four-seater aeroplane at Wilson Airport and with two ladies as extra passengers we headed north. One of the ladies was a horse rider and through the District Officer in Maralal I arranged for four horses to be made available to us and to await us at the rough airstrip just outside Maralal village. The plan was then that we would ride to Naibor Enkeju and camp with the ladies taking care of the horses while Rusty and I climbed.

The flight took us to the west of Mount Kenya and over Naro Moru where I had a friend – Mickie Fernandez who farmed nearby. I was aware that Mickie had an airstrip on his farm and in a phone call to him, he suggested that we landed for a coffee *en route*. I asked him for details of his airstrip – its exact position, length and condition. He arranged to be on the airstrip at around the time we would be over flying and to indicate by waving if he felt the surface would be all right for us to land.

In excellent weather it took us forty-five minutes from Nairobi to be overhead Mickie's farm near Naro Moru where we had some difficulty locating the airstrip. Concentrating on the search, I was turning and banking the aeroplane and taking little notice of the passengers. All was not well with the two ladies who were becoming airsick into a plastic bag they had found. Rusty by my side and assisting with the search also became unwell. I was unaware of what was going on until I sensed Rusty turning quickly round and saying with some urgency, "Pass the puke bag!" I levelled the aeroplane immediately and apologised for my inconsiderate flying. Eventually we found the airstrip with Mickie gesticulating. I was uncertain of his message and since the strip looked short to me, to avoid further turning, we decided not to land so we climbed to calmer conditions and continued to Maralal.

At Maralal airstrip, there was the "syce" with four horses. I had only limited experience of horse riding and I believe both Rusty and one of the ladies had never been on horseback! We left it to the syce, who knew the horses to allocate our mounts. There was a large black stallion which the syce thought would suit Rusty! With the syce holding it, he mounted in what I felt was an acceptable manner and demonstration of courage, but immediately the syce let go, the horse bolted, with Rusty, arms around its neck disappearing down the runway in a cloud of dust. Somehow, he managed to stay on and turn it round to come tearing back and shoot past us before getting control. It was a fine demonstration and the rest of us gingerly took charge of our mounts to then ride to Naibor Enkeju where we had a great

Four horses awaited us at the Maralal airstrip (large black stallion in the middle). The aeroplane had been pushed into the "bush hangar" to be protected from the tropical sun. (The pole holding up the roof had first to be removed and then replaced.)

weekend with some new routes on the rock, followed by an uneventful flight back to Nairobi.

My work in Kenya had been as an Agricultural Officer with the Colonial Service, teaching the cultivation of tropical crops in the African Reserve. The work came to an end on Kenya's Independence in December 1963 and I returned to the United Kingdom to search for work there.

123

Top: Naibor Enkeju
Above: B Cliff on Naibor Enkeju
Right: R Baillie on Naibor Enkeju

Since all of my agricultural experience had been dealing with tropical crops, I found it difficult to get work in temperate agriculture and a number of interviews failed to materialise into an offer of employment. My thoughts turned to aviation and since I had a background in agriculture I made enquiries into crop-spraying with aircraft. A Commercial Pilot's Licence was mandatory, but before the exams for the Licence could be taken, a minimum of two hundred flying hours was required. With my flying in Kenya I already had one hundred and twenty hours, so I enrolled on a Commercial Pilot's course to convert these hours into a C.P.L. at Oxford Airport with instructions in instrument flying and with the intention of joining a crop-spraying firm.

On gaining a C.P.L. I joined "Farm-Air" at Southampton Airport and started to enjoy landing on and working from unprepared fields, rather like bush flying in Kenya. It was very challenging flying and provided the adventure I craved for after life in Kenya.

Some months later it all came to a very sudden end ...

Crop spraying and the accident

On 13th April 1965 I flew a Piper Cub, adapted for agricultural flying with the tank for granular fertilizer replacing the rear passenger seat and situated immediately behind the pilot's seat (a Piper Cub has two seats in tandem), from Southampton to a Warminster farm in Wiltshire. I landed on the selected field where our loader, who had driven there earlier in the day from Southampton was waiting with the necessary loading equipment.

Loaded with four to five hundredweight of granular fertilizer on each flight, I top-dressed the required fields at a height of about twenty feet, with each flight taking about five minutes. It was undulating terrain but not particularly difficult flying. The operation took about six hours and by the end of the afternoon I was rather tired as the evening light altered conditions somewhat.

The last field was in a valley with a wood at one end, the farmer requiring the two sides of the valley to be top-dressed. I elected to treat the field by starting at the top of the valley sides and fly along the contour towards the wood, climbing over it at the end of each run, then turning and returning to work my way down the hillside in the same direction of flight. On the very last treatment flight I completed the valley floor and climbed over the wood. There my memory remains a blank. The loader, immediately realising something had gone wrong when I did not return started a search and once it had been established that an accident had occurred, he telephoned Farm-Air and spoke to the Director. The Director's first response was to ask what the aeroplane was like whereupon the loader replied, "It's a write-off and Barry is in more or less the same state!"

By chance, a gamekeeper was in the wood and he heard the aeroplane passing over periodically, followed by the noise of

Two views of the aircraft after the accident

the accident. He was the first person to the scene which was in the field after the wood in the direction of flight. Weekslater he visited me in the hospital and described what took place.

He had heard the noise of a faltering engine followed by a crash and then silence, to then come out of the wood to look. He found the crashed aircraft with me trapped inside, covered in blood and fuel. I had removed my crash helmet and was conscious and in turning my head towards him warned him not to touch anything because of the fire risk and that care should be taken in getting me out because my back was broken. He then left to alert the emergency services.

At the accident in Wiltshire the fire service was called to cut me out of the wreckage with an attendant doctor to administer morphine. The doctor later told me that even with the morphine I had refused to pass out until I had instructed them which struts to cut and how to get me out. Only after that did I lapse into unconsciousness.

My next recollection was being wheeled lying flat, face up on a trolley through a hospital door and seeing the sign above, "Salisbury General Hospital" in a brief second of consciousness. I was taken into the intensive care unit, initially for a week before then on to a ward of men where I was suffering from amnesia for three to four weeks before one day suddenly regaining normality. Those three to four weeks are a blank in my mind but I will record what I later learned from the nurses and fellow bed-mates.

After the period in intensive care, the doctors felt that it would be beneficial for me to be in male company to join in the banter which goes on. I was wheeled into the male orthopaedic ward where there were men of all ages recovering from bone fractures in various accidents. I was allocated a bed half-way down the ward and next to a pig farmer with broken bones. In a corner bed was a man called Reg who had been driving a lorry collecting milk churns. With one foot on the lorry and one on the milk stand, he had got a full milk churn half-way across when the stand collapsed, resulting in him falling onto his back with the milk churn on his stomach. He had broken his back and was lying flat, face up in the corner bed. He was a vociferous man with a loud voice and it soon became apparent to me that he was the "barrack room lawyer" (a naval term for the man on the mess deck who always tries to assume command and be the spokesman for the more subdued shipmates). It appears that I soon took exception to his noise and shouted at him to "shut it". He threatened immediately to come across and sort me out and asked who was this upstart who was threatening his authority. I was described as a crashed pilot with a broken back and thereafter he exhibited a strong distaste for me; neither of us, of course, were fit enough for battle. It was said by the pig farmer that whenever I was in periods of violent pain, my temperament changed and I became aggressive, even to the matron and nurses attending me or anyone else coming near to the bed, particularly if sitting on it and causing vibration in my back.

Rusty Baillie came in with John Cleare, Rusty telling me that I was signed up as a mountain guide on the Matterhorn centenary celebrations and "to get fit fast". Apparently I had also devised a plan for them to get me out of hospital with a system of ladders and rope, but they left me in there! My imagination must have been running rife! It was reported by an elderly sailor friend of mine who came in with his wife that I told them a horrific story of how I was being treated. I told them that each day I was being strapped to a pole and turned over and over as on a spit, to keep my back straight. It must have sounded authentic for he left with his wife in tears at the suffering I had reputedly to undergo. The matron had confirmed to him, however, that I talked "a load of rubbish". Quite suddenly, after almost three weeks of this behaviour, the amnesia abruptly stopped when I turned to the pig farmer and asked what was going on, my whereabouts and in particular who was shaving me? He said, "You are in Salisbury hospital, you've been next to me for three weeks, creating havoc when you are in pain and shaving yourself!" I couldn't believe the stories he told me about my behaviour. One was confirmed that very night when the nurses came round to hand out evening drinks. At the foot of the bed, a young nurse with a black eye asked me what I would like to drink. I replied, "Hot chocolate", and then she said, "I'll make it but I'm not coming near you, Barry Cliff." "What is your problem?" I asked. "You", she said, "I came to the bed last night with the hot chocolate. You knocked it out of my hand and gave me this eye!" I apologised profusely and had to do also to the matron for inappropriate behaviour.

Mr Brock, my surgeon, felt that it was best to simply allow me to rest and get over the shock once I had recovered from the amnesia and during that time he consulted with other surgeons, particularly some in Newcastle who had dealt with injuries similar to mine in miners from that area. (Lumbar vertebrae 1, 2 and 3 were crushed with consequent damage to the left leg nerves.) His eventual decision was not to attempt any surgery, risking further nerve damage but to encase me in plaster for six weeks to see how the crushed vertebrae settled down. For the plaster procedure I was suspended from a hook by stretched-up arms with the operator walking round and round me unwinding the plaster, resulting in me being encased from chest to hip. In that state, I lay in bed for five weeks until one day I was told I would be stood for a few seconds. I had ambitions to walk to the toilet and scorned the few seconds story. The moment I was vertical I keeled over, unable even to stand! It was described as "quite normal" after being horizontal for so long. Thereafter was a long period of daily attempts to improve, eventually managing a few steps. I graduated to a wheel-chair since my leg muscles had wasted away and embarked on a long period of physiotherapy to regain some muscle whilst still a patient at the hospital.

After a number of months recovering I did learn to walk again and soon after discharge from the hospital I elected to undergo a medical examination at the Directorate of Civil Aviation in order to re-validate my flying licence. I was in really poor shape and, little wonder, failed the medical. The examining doctor, however, was ex-R.A.F. and he knew of the R.A.F. rehabilitation centre at Headley Court, Epsom, for injured service personnel. The early ejector seats apparently often resulted in crushed vertebrae to R.A.F. pilots, injuries such as mine. He managed to have me admitted to the centre as a full-time civilian patient and I then underwent three months of intensive physiotherapy and exercise in the purpose-built establishment, also with very good food.

Apart from the excellent professional treatment, with even a very warm swimming pool to swim in, it was good fun living with other men and pilots, and a fine camaraderie developed. There were also one or two other commercial pilots. One in particular was Val Croft, a then B.O.A.C. Comet captain, who at visitors' time was always visited by a bevy of air-hostesses. His favourite joke was to point me out to them and comment, "You see that fellow over there: he flew into a tree" – not true of course but presumably expressing his disdain of "crop-sprayers". He had lost his licence when his legs were crushed whilst walking between two parked cars outside Heathrow Airport when one shot forward at speed, trapping him between the two bumpers. Another commercial pilot, however, a 747 captain with Cathy Pacific, on meeting me commented that, "it's nice to meet a *real* pilot!" (maybe also in jest).

A Piper Cub, adapted for crop-spraying, was never an ideal aircraft. In an accident, with the tank (or hopper as it is called) immediately behind the pilot, he is trapped between the engine and hopper and, as in my case the weight being carried shoots forwards and pushes him into the instrument panel. With wing fuel tanks above him on either side, the fuel is also dangerously placed. With these aspects to overcome, Piper designed a much safer specialised aircraft in the Piper Pawnee. The hopper is in *front* of the pilot and being a low winged monoplane, the fuel tanks *below* and outboard of him. In fact the pilot is nearer to the tail than the propeller and the cockpit is mounted on top of the fuselage, enabling excellent all-round visibility, so critical in low level flying with all the weight in front of him.

132

Some time after this accident, this time *in* a Piper Pawnee I had gone through some wires when spraying potatoes in Lincolnshire. The wire cutters located in the leading edges of the undercarriage cut the wires, assisted by the propeller, causing a blue flash in the cockpit. I had immediately used the dump lever in the Pawnee to instantly discharge the load in seconds, shooting the aeroplane vertically upwards twenty feet to safety. The trick is, of course, to survey the field to be sprayed *beforehand* and to look for posts, since the wires are very difficult to detect when travelling at speed and looking downwards. Even that doesn't always work in your favour. A friend of mine was spraying a field of beans in Tanzania which had a narrow line of trees on the side from which he approached the field. He flew over the trees and descended to the field on each run. Halfway along there was a gap in the trees, wide enough to take the aeroplane, making him decide to go through the gap at that particular point rather than having to descend each time to get to "spray height". There were wires across the gap which he hadn't noticed since the posts were in the trees. The wires inverted the aeroplane and dumped it in the field where it exploded into flames, killing him instantly.

On leaving Headley Court and considerably fitter, I underwent the medical examination again and this time was passed fit enough to regain my licence, almost a year to the day after the accident.

Chapter 9

Adventures in Aviation 2

de Havilland Rapide

Searching for work again, I replied to an advertisement for a pilot wanted for a de Havilland *Rapide* twin-engined bi-plane for operating pleasure flights. I was accepted and took the required tests to qualify to fly that lovely old "wood and fabric" aeroplane initially at Land's End in Cornwall and later at Swansea Airport operating ten-minute pleasure flights over the Gower Peninsular with eight passengers. Some time later and living near Netheravon airfield at the time I was aware of the de Havilland *Rapide* which periodically landed there. It belonged to the Red Devils Parachute Display Team and I was told that they required a pilot from time to time. Since I was then an experienced pilot on a *Rapide* they periodically asked me to fly their aeroplane. All the seats were taken out and with the passenger door off, eight parachutists could be carried. It was made quite clear to me that although they enjoyed their parachuting, none of them

Above: The Red Devils' de Havilland Rapide
Right: Three of the Red Devils team

135

liked flying and that the sooner the aeroplane got to their minimum jumping height (1,200 ft) the happier they were, only then did they feel relaxed and in control since in the event of a problem they could always jump out! Since they were also paying for flying time, the sooner the aeroplane got down after they jumped, the better. In fact I was told that some pilots were capable of getting the aircraft down before the parachutists themselves had reached the ground!

Most of the time they required a pilot, it was to operate the aeroplane for practice jumps at their own airstrip, but once they had a display to do near Hull which involved a ferry flight of about two hours from Netheraven to Brough. Some of the team were to go up by train, but others were apparently happy to come in the aeroplane. In good weather the flight up to Brough passed without incident as did some spectacular parachute displays around Hull. On the return flight to Netheavon two days later, however, the weather had deteriorated. Nevertheless, some of the team wished to come on the ferry flight. In a *Rapide* the pilot sits in the small nose cone, half isolated from the passengers by a partition with a small door, often left open. With an empty fuselage without the passenger door and passengers strung out across the floor, the pilot can easily sense any movement or change of position behind. Once again, on the flight up to operating height I could sense tension but with a few glances back, all seemed calm once we were established on the compass course and level flight south. The aeroplane was not equipped for instrument flight and after a quarter of an hour we were obliged to descend to keep clear of cloud and remain under VFR. I sensed movement and unease behind, followed shortly by a tap on the shoulder. It was the sergeant wanting to know where we were. The map was spread out on my knee and I indicated our position. To my surprise he then turned round to the others and calmly announced, "He says he doesn't know." He then asked me to fly above the main railway line south and advised me that the boys would be jumping out and leaving me in order to take the train back home if we flew any lower. We managed to maintain altitude and they appeared very relieved to get their feet on the ground at Netheravon.

Guyana

Searching for a more stable and regular employment and after an interview in the London head office, I was eventually offered employment with Bookers, a large sugar estate company in Guyana, South America, as a pilot/agronomist on a two-year contract. I understood this would involve being based on one of the estates working in the laboratory as a technician analysing sugar cane, examining the crop itself and determining the treatment that would be required for pest control or the top-dressing of nutrients by aircraft. I would then be required to fly the company's crop-spraying aircraft in treating the sugar cane. It sounded a challenging and interesting position but travelling out by sea I received a very cool reception on reporting to the Guyana office in Georgetown. In fact the authorities there seemed unaware of the position I had been offered by their head office in London and there was some discussion as to the work I would be expected to do. The manager of the estate to which I was

Spraying sugar cane in a Piper Pawnee in Guyana.

eventually posted made it quite clear that he had little time for university graduates and that in his opinion the only way to learn about sugar cane cultivation was the way he had done, i.e. as a labourer doing all the types of work involved, eventually qualifying for management positions.

On walking round the blocks of sugar cane I was soon aware that senior staff were all issued with Land Rovers. Requesting to see the manager to comment on my lack of transport, he looked out of the window and spotted a mule. "You see that?" he said, "I had to ride one of those when I started" and he seemed to feel that it would be quite appropriate for me also. However, he finally arranged for a motorcycle! The reception from the Chief Pilot was not a great deal different and he appeared to feel that I was not the right person to join his team of himself and one other pilot to fly the aircraft, treating the completely flat sugar cane fields of the estate. Nevertheless, he gave me some training and I was eventually allowed to top-dress and spray the company's sugar estates. There had clearly been little liaison between the London head office and the management in the field and accordingly I suffered the consequences. The agronomists appeared to resent the fact that I could also fly and the Chief Pilot appeared to resent my dual qualifications. I certainly enjoyed riding the motorcycle and flying the aircraft when the chance arose, but I sensed the embarrassment I had become to Senior Management and was pleased to be eventually called in to be offered a "separation".

I took it gladly and was immediately offered partnership with an American to join a bush flying operation with a de Havilland Beaver on floats. I had noticed this aircraft moored to a floating jetty in the Demerara River, and knowing little of the interior of the country at that time it had really fired my imagination. I flew as co-pilot for a number of flights with an experienced Canadian float-plane pilot and learned the fascinating techniques of water handling on some narrow fast-flowing rivers. I soon realised the importance of his first question some before we ever got into the aircraft when he asked if I had any sailing or boating experience. He eventually considered me competent for a sea-plane rating to my Guyanese flying licence.

The Beaver float plane with a canoe attached to the port float struts

Bush Flying

Operating then as a single pilot, adventure really started. There were no navigational aids in the interior and the only map available was rather rudimentary. Guyana is a land full of rivers and the name itself means "land of many waters" in the Amerindian languages. Apart from the narrow coastal strip of agricultural land where the main crops of sugar and rice are grown, the remainder of the country is tropical forest but with cattle ranching on areas of highland savannah in the interior. There are alluvial gold and diamond deposits in the rivers of the forested areas and much of the flying involved carrying supplies and prospectors to the workings of these two minerals. In Guyana these prospectors are called "pork knockers", a name resulting from their diet of salted pork and many young men in Georgetown had at some stage of their lives attempted to seek their fortunes prospecting in the interior. Diving in the rivers for diamonds from a raft and using

Operating over thick tropical forest intersperseed with rivers

a simple compressed-air line was very hazardous and there were accidents and deaths. To me they were a fine group of tough, happy, hard-living men, and I very much enjoyed being connected with their adventurous lives. They would go into the "workings" or "claims" for a few months, then return to Georgetown, often drink away the profits and then ask to be flown back in again. Sometimes they would ask to be taken to new stretches of river deep in the forested interior and this would involve careful, fascinating float-plane flying into new river workings. The stretch of river where they wished to prospect had to be over-flown and from an aerial assessment confirm there was enough depth, length and width (50 ft wing span for the Beaver) to make a safe alighting and takeoff. Deep in the forest with trees and thick vegetation on all river banks it was necessary to carry a boat so that after alighting, the

141

aeroplane would first be anchored in mid-river and the bank accessed by boat. An area for the prospectors could then be cleared and a pontoon made for the float-plane to get alongside and unload freight and also enabling the aeroplane to be turned round by man-handling.

My prospector passengers all had great character as one would expect and they learned to trust my judgement and ability as much as I trusted them. Sometimes, being without money, they would request to be flown in free of charge, with the promise of payment on return when they "struck lucky". I was sometimes offered a diamond for the fare back to Georgetown, but not knowing the value of a rough diamond or even being interested in them I asked for cash. My trust waivered once when on agreeing to fly four men to a new claim on a river close to the Venezuelan boarder, an incident occurred. Soon after takeoff from the Demerara River next to Georgetown Timehri Airport, the radio controller called me with the aeroplane call sign and asked if one of my passengers was named Cowboy. I turned round to face the passengers, all of whom had heard the question. A swarthy thick-set man gave me a wicked smile and announced that he indeed was Cowboy and I noticed right away that he had a diamond set in each of his front teeth. I duly reported to the control tower that Cowboy was on board. I was then told to return immediately to our river base and I started to bank the aeroplane to comply. Cowboy clearly knew what was going on and in displaying a gun indicated that he and his team wished to go straight ahead to their agreed destination. I understood immediately what he meant and with an equally wicked smile felt it was more diplomatic to switch the radio off and return back on the compass course. Cowboy nodded gratefully and thanked me again with his smile for understanding. The rest of the flight was uneventful but on return to Georgetown I was called in to the Control Tower to explain why I had not complied with the request to return. In sympathy with Cowboy I did not mention the gun but made the lame excuse that the message had been misinterpreted. He was apparently required to answer police questioning.

Guyana has in its interior one of the world's great waterfalls. One hour's flying from Georgetown is the natural wonder of Kaieteur Falls (right) where the 400 ft wide Potaro River plunges over the Pakaraima Plateau in a stunning 741 ft single drop (five times the height of Niagara). It is a big tourist attraction with its remoteness and won-derful colouring. It is a foam-rich cataract but plunges over the edge in a mass of golden brown and amber which changes to cream, pink and saffron as it falls while the rising vapour veils it in clouds of prismatic hues and the glorious ever-changing rainbow.

Above: The Beaver take-off from the top of the falls (photo: Peter Hood)
Below: The colour of the falls at the lip

With seven tourists on board the float-plane it was a special adventure to alight on the river above the Falls and from our camp and clearing 300 metres from the brink they could walk along the track to the very lip of the Fall. The takeoff from the top of the Falls never failed to delight and thrill the tourists but there was one thrill too many for me once when I was fortunately alone. I had flown 1,200 lbs of freight for prospectors to our camp at the top of the Falls, and taxied back up-river for takeoff. Approaching the lip of the Falls at full power and

144

almost airborne, there was a loud bang in the engine bay. With the engine still functioning I managed to get airborne and immediately got sufficient height to bank the aircraft and return to the river above the Falls. It was then that I noticed flames coming from under the cowling. I immediately put the aircraft down on the river opposite our camp and jumped out on the port float and threw out the anchor. With the lack of forward speed the flames seemed to be really taking hold and I felt there would be an explosion. After making sure all switches and fuel were turned off I suddenly realised that I was confronted by either getting burnt, or a swim in the river with piranha fish. I chose to risk the fish and dived off the float and swam to our camp. On reaching the bank I looked back at the aeroplane to see plenty of smoke but the flames had gone out. Eventually I swam back when all seemed well so that I could use the radio, which I found still worked to call for our engineer to be flown out. On arrival he found that the catchment bowl under the carburettor had been flooded and had caught fire when the engine back-fired. It had fortunately burnt itself out and apart from some burnt wiring there was little other damage. We had been lucky not to lose the aeroplane.

Operation "El Dorado"

In January 1970 I was approached by Dr Jevan Berrangé who was leading Operation "El Dorado", a British Government sponsored Technical Co-operation project involving the primary geological mapping of southern Guyana, a largely uninhabited region covered by tropical rainforest where rivers form the only travel access routes. Jevan's plan was to use a Guyana Airways D.C.3 to fly in all the men, equipment, food and canoes from Georgetown to Apoteri, an Amerindian village in the centre of Guyana where there was a suitable airstrip and a landing pool alongside on the Rupununi River below. The final expedition (1970) in the far southeast of Guyana was dependant on flying in the canoes attached to the struts of a float-plane, based on Jevan's experience in Canada where he had done similar work with a float-plane. He approached a number of other pilots, but none was prepared to undertake the work. He reports that he was "lucky enough to make contact with you and was greatly relieved to find someone with enough *cojones* to undertake the challenge of lashing a canoe to the struts of the Beaver, flying in the far south and alighting on previously unscouted relatively small pools in rivers."

His plan was for me to fly two expedition groups to their respective starting-off points, one led by Jevan and the other by his colleague, another British geologist, Dr Richard Johnson. The expedition teams would then canoe down the rivers, conducting their geological survey *en route* and I would then pick them up a couple of months later at a pre-arranged rendezvous, where obviously the rivers would be larger and clearly easier to access with the Beaver.

His plan worked well and the two teams were duly flown to their respective starting points, Richard to the headwaters of the New River and Jevan to the headwaters of the Oronoque River.

146

Above: The canoe on the port float. I always tied it on myself and always on the port float so I could keep an eye on it from the pilot's seat.
Below: Bush jetty built by the three Amerindians in ½ hour to enable the Beaver to moor alongside the bank (photo: J Berrangé)

The narrow river was marginal for the 50 foot wingspan (photo: J Berrangé)

Some weeks later Jevan radioed in asking me to evacuate him and his team from the Kutari River. His small aluminium canoe was painted "Day-Glo" orange on the underside and I was instructed to fly up-river and look for the upturned canoe on the true left bank, where he felt there was sufficient space for the Beaver to alight and take off. It was an area new to me and well isolated to the south of the country. His instructions were accurate and after a very long solo ferry flight over dense bush, I found his camp and the canoe without much difficulty. Overflying and assessing the river, however, it appeared to me to be short and very fast-flowing; just down-river from the chosen area there was an angry-looking rapid and above the selected site was a small waterfall. I made two low-level passes and on the third a gentle touch-down opposite Jevan and his team. I had to use the throttle to hold the aircraft in to the current before eventually shutting down the engine and leaping out onto the port float to anchor the aeroplane. I immediately realised just how fast the current was. Once the anchor took hold the port float dipped in the current and I felt the strain on the anchor line which I had made fast to the cleat on the forward end of the float. As I looked at it stretching and straining, the rope suddenly snapped and the aeroplane, spinning round in the middle of the river started to career down-river. I had visions of ending up in the rocky rapids where the aeroplane would have undoubtedly been badly smashed. I hastily jumped back into the cockpit to start the engine, which fortunately fired up immediately, enabling me to regain control and taxi back up-river. Choosing a quiet corner with less current and opposite Jevan's camp, I carefully taxied the aeroplane in and with then no anchor available, put the port wing gently into the overhanging branches in order to hold the aircraft by climbing on the wing and holding the branches by hand until Jevan came across in his boat to assist. We then loaded the Beaver and lashed his canoe onto the port struts so I could keep an eye on it from the pilot's position. Knowing how short the strip was and also of the waterfall upstream in the direction of takeoff, we were operating on the margins of the possible.

Once we had loaded the aeroplane and taxied the short distance down-river, I instructed Jevan to keep a lookout on the starboard side of the aircraft as I opened the throttle for full power and to indicate when we were alongside fuel drums

*View on the Potaro River before turning for take-off. It was necessary to get the starboard wing **under** the obvious overhanging branch*

at the water edge of his camp. If not airborne by then I would abort the take-off; this duly happened. I'm not sure how I looked as we taxied back but Jevan was somewhat paler than usual in spite of having a good tan after three months of canoeing. We off-loaded some freight and Jevan stayed with two men to be picked up in a proposed second flight. After taking three of his Amerindian crew with equipment and a canoe out to Apoteri I returned, but as it was then late in the afternoon I overnighted with him at his camp. We chatted round the camp fire about our adventurous lives and the subject of survival was raised. Jevan asked me what equipment I carried in the event of coming down in the bush. I had very little apart from an axe, rope and flotation gear with the intention of getting down from the trees, making my way to a river and going down that, always assuming no serious injury. It was then that he stated that he carried a .22 revolver which he would throw away as with the expedition coming to an end, he had no further use for it. He offered it to me and it was put with a few rounds of ammunition into the back locker of the Beaver and there it remained for a considerable time. This was his last camp in southern Guyana and I was sorry that Operation "El Dorado" had come to an end and that I would have no further opportunity to work with such fine men as Jevan and Richard.

I did not experience the same sentiments with an American prospector who contacted our company and asked for assistance to transfer a large engine from his camp on one river over to the big Essequibo River. I enquired about the size and weight of the engine and although uncertain of these required figures, he commented that it had been flown in some time ago with a Beaver float-plane (as ours). Accordingly I duly flew down to his camp to find a huge compressor engine sitting on a makeshift raft in the river. It looked enormous but once again I was reassured that it had been delivered there by Beaver float-plane. By taking off both the port and starboard passenger doors, we eventually manhandled it into the aircraft whereupon the aeroplane suddenly tipped backwards with the forward ends of the floats pointing skywards and the aft ends under water. We balanced the aeroplane and tied the engine down and alone I taxied out into mid-river for the take-off. On opening the throttle I soon realised that the aeroplane was severely overloaded and it took a lot of river to eventually get "on the step" and to gently coax the aeroplane into the air with a gentle turn to the Essequibo. At the Essequibo the American was waiting at a raft in mid-river where once again we managed to tip the aeroplane backwards when trying to off-load the engine.

On telling the American that the aeroplane had been grossly overloaded and that his engine had certainly not been flown in a Beaver float-plane he calmly said, "Barry, I believe you are right. It could have been a de Havilland *Otter*." (a much bigger aircraft with a far greater payload). We parted company and thankfully he never used us again.

We had a number of fuel caches in 44-gallon drums in the bush, most of which had to be flown in with the Beaver which could only carry three drums at a time and which were difficult to load and discharge. There was, however, one major bush road into the interior which crossed the lower reaches of the Potaro River by a steel girder bridge, built by a Scottish engineer and called the Garroway Stream crossing. It was a very convenient place to enable us to take in a larger number of fuel drums at one time by lorry to a fuel cache at the side of the bridge crossing. With a plentiful supply of fuel and a suitable river on which to alight and take off it was a good staging point for flights further into the interior of the country. It was a fascinating point for operating with the Beaver! For sufficient suitable river length, it was necessary to taxi back up-stream, under the bridge, through a right-angled bend immediately after the bridge before then turning round to

Main picture: The steel girder bridge at Garroway Stream

Right: The right-angled bend, then under the bridge for take-off

Below: View from the bridge parapet of the Beaver at full power (photo: GS Cliff - my father)

begin the take-off. With full power and still on the water the aeroplane had then to be coaxed round the right-angled bend (in float-plane technique terms called "on the step", i.e. with the floats just skimming on the surface), then under the bridge before take-off speed was attained.

Our base in the Demerara River, near Georgetown the capital, was a simple floating jetty made from oil drums and planks of wood. Here we loaded freight, passengers and moored and refuelled the aeroplane. On return from flights, it was my custom to overfly the base to alert our ground crew and engineer to be ready to "catch" the aeroplane as it was taxied in (a float-plane has no brakes and the engine is cut some distance off and the aeroplane judged to still have sufficient "way" to reach the jetty). Returning one day from a long flight into the interior and overflying the base, I was surprised to see a number of policemen standing on the jetty amongst our ground crew. I duly landed and taxied in, to be immediately boarded by the police who advised me that they would search the aeroplane! Of course they found the gun and ammunition in the rear locker and I was immediately arrested and escorted back to Georgetown despite my objections with those also of the ground crew. At Georgetown police station the accusation was explained to me as "gun running" and I was put in a police cell for the night. Explaining my hunger after a day's flying I was treated as a real criminal and a bowl of rice was passed under the door some time later. With time to reflect, I remembered our competitor's loader helping with the Beaver at Garroway Stream and he must have looked in the locker and seen the gun. The competitor (an American called Mitch who operated both a helicopter and a Cessna 206 float-plane) had exhibited antagonism a number of times and I was aware of his opposition to our much greater payload and ability to fly in all weathers. He doubtless saw an opportunity to create trouble for us. Trouble it was, for we were immediately grounded with the operator's licence revoked. After the night in the cell I was let out and immediately visited the British Consulate. After explaining what had taken place I was treated rather like a naughty schoolboy and abruptly told that I "shouldn't have carried the gun." They were clearly annoyed at having their peace disturbed and were unsympathetic and no help whatsoever with my predicament. I took on a local lawyer but it was a long drawn out procedure much to the delight of the competitor. Whilst it was being resolved I returned by sea on a tanker to the U.K. to attend my sister's wedding and eventually received communication that I would be allowed to return and continue operating. My trust had been shattered, however, and I decided not to return, later joining a crop-spraying firm in the south of England for the summer.

Beaver take-off

155

Chapter 10

Adventures in Aviation 3

Crop-spraying in the U.K. and Return to Kenya safari flying

Exciting flying, spraying small fields, hardly matched handling a float-plane in tropical bush and at the end of that summer I returned to Kenya to join a flying safari firm in Mombasa taking tourists into the game parks. It was whilst there that I heard of the new international airport built in the Seychelles and it occurred to me that with the expected influx of tourists and no airstrip on any of the other islands within the Seychelles, that there would be a potential for a float-plane operation within the islands.

The Seychelles

Accordingly I flew across to the Seychelles to meet with the newly appointed Director of Aviation with a proposal for an Operator's Licence. Regrettably only one licence was available and it had already been granted to a company in Nairobi for a wheeled inter-island light aircraft operation with an initial proposal to build an airstrip on the neighbouring island of Praslin. On return to Kenya and at the Director's suggestion to meet with the company in Nairobi I visited them and attempted to persuade the company to operate a float-plane as being more suitable and without the expense of building airstrips for wheeled aircraft. With no experience of float-planes, the Director was very reluctant to become involved but to my surprise he offered me the position of starting his operation as pilot/manager in the Seychelles. As, with my persuasion, he had offered a possible expansion into float-planes once the operation had become established, I accepted and accompanied him on a delivery flight from Nairobi to the Seychelles in a Piper Twin Seneca.

The Piper Twin Seneca on arrival at the Seychelles and ready to start operating

On arrival there I was left alone to build up the business initially with single ten-minute pleasure flights from Mahe Airport until the proposed new airstrip on Praslin was completed. After the initial twelve-minute flight from Mahe to Praslin and a successful landing on the new rough airstrip, business accumulated. Tourists and local Seychelloise were then pleased to fly between the two islands – it being no longer necessary to go by sea on the infamous *Lady Esme* with its renowned sea-sickness-making wallowing in the sea. It was a fascinating place to live and operate amongst lovely island people. With only Mahe and Praslin available for the aircraft and in an attempt to

158

expand the business, an airstrip was planned for Bird Island some distance away to the north. A problem developed with the Seneca however, and the aeroplane had to be grounded with a cracked port wing spar. With such short flights it seemed unnecessary to operate an aircraft with retractable undercarriage and it was decided to change the Seneca for a Britten Norman Islander ten-seater with a fixed undercarriage. After only a few flights with this aircraft I was amazed to have a visit from the company director with some surprising news. His recently qualified son was to take over the operation, float-plane plans were to be scrapped and I was requested to leave. My dedication and efforts had been in vain and I left for Kenya to accept a cotton-spraying contract in Burundi, Central Africa, for three months before then returning to Mombasa to fly for Air Kenya again with a Piper Seneca flying tourists to the Serengeti, Zanzibar, Lamu and Amboseli.

Flying tourists in a Piper Seneca on the airstrip at the lip of the Serengeti Ngoro Ngoro crater

Return to University

It may sound an idyllic lifestyle but I tired of flying tourists in an aircraft owned by someone else and there seemed to be no future for me. In an attempt to return to my main profession of tropical agriculture I visited the U.K. and arranged to see the Professor of Agriculture at Leeds University where I had qualified twenty-five years earlier. The Professor remembered me and was surprised and I suspect disappointed that I was employed as a "bush pilot" and not a director of agriculture somewhere abroad. He considered that in order for me to return to agriculture I should update my agricultural knowledge by returning to a University course. He suggested that a newly-opened course at Reading University for one year, leading to an MSc (Crop Protection) would be a suitable direction to pursue, particularly with my experience in crop protection with aircraft. Deciding to follow his advice I returned to Kenya to finalise my affairs before embarking on the course at Reading and changing a lifestyle from a house on the beach at Mombasa to a one-bedroom flat in Reading at the on-set of winter. It was a drastic change and for the first Autumn term I had great difficulty in settling down to study again. By the Christmas vacation and with an academic project to do I decided to abscond and I returned to Kenya and Mombasa to fly safaris again in order to earn money for the University course. It was a rash decision as at the start of term again in January I had to re-adapt once more.

When all the younger students on the MSc course were questioned by the Professor at the first lecture of the Winter term I was embarrassed to have to admit that I had spent the vacation working in East Africa bush flying, instead of preparing a thesis. This created a great cheer amongst my fellow students - all of whom had listened to my weak explanation! He was not impressed and I was told I should be more serious in my approach if I wished to be considered for the qualification. With more interesting subjects to study for the Winter term I adapted better and was eventually successful in qualifying for the MSc (Crop Protection).

World Health Organisation and River Blindness

Prior to the end of term a representative of the World Health Organisation in Geneva came to lecture to the course and he talked about some of the Health Programmes the organisation was involved in. I must clearly have stood out from the rest of the class as a mature student and after the lecture he approached me and asked why I was on the course. He was very interested in my background of agriculture in Africa and particularly my age and experience as a qualified crop-spraying pilot with aircraft. He then told me of the WHO River Blindness Campaign in West Africa and that the organisation had been looking for some time for a person with qualifications such as mine to run the aerial operations of the Programme. Some time later I was asked to attend an interview at the WHO headquarters in Geneva and was eventually offered the position of Chief of Aerial Operations for the Programme to be based in Ouagadougou, Upper Volta, West Africa.

It was made clear to me that the position was a managerial one to ensure the best interests of the WHO and the Onchocerciasis Control Programme in the Volta River Basin by the supervision of an aerial contractor together with pilots and engineers. In this respect I would not be required to act as pilot but merely to supervise the aerial operations. The Programme was already in its early stages in 1976 when I accepted and was flown out to Upper Volta (now Burkina Faso) to work with a team of very dedicated people on the huge humane and fascinating programme.

River Blindness (Onchocerciasis) is a parasitic disease of the tropics which in particular affected much of West Africa. It is a devastating and debilitating disease caused by thread-like worms (microfilariae) found in nodules under the skin and spread by the bite of the female blackfly (simulium damnosum) when it requires a blood meal in order to develop its eggs. The blackfly, present in their thousands, lay their eggs in fast-flowing rivers (white-water rapids) where there is plenty of oxygenation. There the eggs hatch and develop into larvae, eventually emerging as adult flies; these then search for a blood meal to infect humans and continue the cycle. The disease was first identified in the 1960s as a major obstacle to socio-economic development in a large part of West Africa, since it prevented human settlement in fertile river valleys of the savannah areas and indeed whole villages migrated away from the valleys because of the association of the disease to the rivers (hence the name River Blindness). In 1976 of an estimated population of 10,000,000 in an area of more than

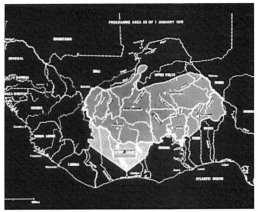

Left: The Programme area of 7 countries: Mali; Ivory Coast; Upper Volta; Ghana; Togo; Benin and Niger (photo: WHO)

Below: West Africa with the 7 countries shown, all river breeding sites treated weekly

Above: A local farmer, totally blind from River Blindness (photo: WHO)

Right: A heavily-infested breeding site (white water) being treated by helicopter

163

1,235,000 km² more than one million were suffering from the disease and 100,000 had serious eye manifestations. In 1976 there was no medical solution to the Onchocerciasis problem. The only method of control of the disease at that time was to attempt to reduce the population of the vector (simulium damnosum) by means of a larvicide applied to the rivers breeding the fly thereby reducing the risk of infection. The larval stage of the fly lasts 7-10 days and it was therefore necessary to treat the rivers on a weekly cycle. At the start of the programme the whole of the savannah portion of the Volta River Basin where the disease was prevalent covered 700,000 km² and encompassed parts of seven countries – Mali; Ivory Coast; Upper Volta; Ghana; Togo; Benin; Niger. It was assumed from the start that to operate satisfactorily over such a huge area it would be vital to use aircraft for the application of the larvicide. Not only was this obvious but it was clear also that only by the use of helicopters could the larvicide be satisfactorily delivered to the smaller, heavily-wooded streams and to the small isolated breeding sites which are a conspicuous feature of the dry season. Consideration was given to the purchase of aircraft by WHO but eventually it was decided that the employment of an experienced aerial contractor specialising in spraying and an international reputation would prove most effective. Even for an experienced operator, West African conditions posed many problems. Communication systems are poor and unreliable, excessive dust causes rapid engine and rotor blade wear and the Harmattan northeast winds give poor visibility making navigation hazardous and high temperatures seriously

Top: Examining river breeding site for larvae with entomologist Frank Walsh (right)

Above: River spraying with the Turbo Thrush aircraft:
Pilot G Gill

Right: Pangalet and B Cliff addressing the crowd from the wing

Top: River spraying with the Hughes 500D helicopter
Above: River spraying with the Hughes 500C helicopter

decrease aircraft performance. All these factors had to be explained and considered by prospective aerial contractors and because the aerial operations had to be carefully geared to the biology of the fly it was imperative that breeding sites received regular weekly treatment without fail. It was hence necessary to negotiate for a strict aerial contract, specific in detail and with a severe penalty clause in the event of default. Writing the aerial contract, sitting on a committee in its award,

166

then overseeing operations were all part of my work. The amount of larvicide used to kill the larvae depended on the volume of water flowing in each river and this had to be calculated weekly by first determining the river discharge and then working out a dosage of larvicide between 0.03 and 0.10 parts per million. A release system from the aircraft had to be designed to enable the pilot to vary the amount released on each river. The development and manufacture of such a system was a further requirement from the aerial contractor.

The aerial operations involved a huge logistical exercise. We specified Hughes 500C or D helicopters as being the most suitable, backed up by two fixed-wing aircraft (Turbo-Thrush) as larger load carriers for treating the bigger rivers particularly in the wet season with a much larger river discharge. Both the fixed-wing and helicopters had an endurance of about 2½ hours and it was therefore necessary to distribute fuel and larvicide caches at strategic sites throughout the programme area. Over one hundred caches were necessary and stocking these in itself had to be a carefully planned exercise, for in the wet season most roads became impassable and the distribution had to be completed before the rains started. A total of 800,000 litres of aviation fuel (Jet A1) and 250,000 litres of larvicide had to be carried by a fleet of lorries to the caches. In the 1976 wet season 18,000 kilometres of river were being treated and surveyed weekly. There were many critical situations, not least when local people soon discovered that Jet A1 aviation fuel was very useful in paraffin cooking stoves and there were instances of pilots finding all the fuel had disappeared at a cache. Although we had negotiated authority to fly across borders between West African countries there were tense situations after numerous political upheavals of *coups d-etats*. When landing in a helicopter at a cache at a border crossing a pilot and myself were held at gunpoint and accused of being mercenaries (we were both bearded) until the Head of State was contacted and our release negotiated.

At its termination of the Programme in 2002 the incidence of the disease had been virtually removed. 30,000,000 people are now protected from infection of the disease, 185,000 have been prevented from going blind and 1.5m have lost the Onchocerciasis infection. It is estimated that a total of 250,000 km² of riverine land is now available for re-settlement and cultivation as a result of the Onchocerciasis control programme operations. Nowadays the development of a successful drug, Ivermectin (one tablet given orally and only once a year), kills the microfilariae, and with the hand treatment of some of the rivers, air operations with helicopters and fixed-wing aircraft are no longer necessary. My work there was for ten years (1976-86) living in the Programme and at the height of operations we operated twelve helicopters and two fixed-wing aircraft with a complement of fourteen pilots, treating the Vector breeding rivers 52 weeks a year, without fail. For me it was fascinating rewarding work and a privilege to be a part of such a successful programme. With all the low-level flying it was hazardous, difficult work and there were many adventurous moments with a fine bunch of pilots, some of whom had flown in the Vietnam War.

It was a costly operation and we flew some 6,000 flight hours each year at about $1,000 per hour. Apart from the flying aspect numerous professional scientists were working for the programme. The finance was handled by the World Bank with a number of donor countries and various agencies asked to contribute. Belgium, Canada, Denmark, France, Germany, Italy, Japan, Korea, Kuwait, Luxembourg, Holland, Portugal, Saudi Arabia, Switzerland, USA, UK all contributed and took a keen interest in how the funds were used and the progress being made to control the disease. So much so that there were periodic visits from their various finance ministers to look at operations in the programme area and witness where their money was being spent. The World Bank's Director of Health Services Dr Bernard Liese went so far as to say, "The spraying is the core operation, going on week after week. If it wasn't for the diligence of the pilots, the programme might fall apart."

The aerial work was the spear head and clearly spectacular to witness. As a result we were often called to give a demonstration whenever the donor representatives visited. Some even asked if they could be a passenger in either helicopter or fixed wing out on operations. I usually attempted to dissuade them for it was hazardous, the pilots understandably reluctant to carry the extra weight and required to talk when concentrating on low level flight. Passengers were not insured and the unpleasant smell of larvicide easily resulted in air sickness. Most of our flying was in the bush and difficult to access on the ground. It was, however, relatively easy to arrange a flying demonstration to view from a bridge over a river being treated. We had a favourite venue on the White Volta river near the African village of Wayen and only one hour's drive on a tarmac

Pangalet, Chief helicopter pilot Bill Riley and B Cliff

road to the west from the headquarters and my office in Ouagadougou. Two colleagues worked with me in aerial operations for the WHO. Jeff Henderickx from Belgium and Pangalet an African from Mali were dedicated workers and between the three of us we usually accompanied a treatment flight each week to instruct the pilots and oversee the work. I would often fly with a new pilot to the programme to make sure he knew how we wanted the larvicide to be deployed and also to teach where all our fuel and larvicide caches were placed.

One week, all the donors were due to visit for an important meeting and the Programme Director called me in with instructions to arrange a larvicide release demonstration. In the previous week a new Canadian fixed wing pilot was taken on by the then Canadian contractor we had and he duly appeared at our weekly briefing (each Monday with the treatment starting every Tuesday). I decided to accompany

170

him the following week. Ian was a young man aged about 25 and claimed to have flown a number of spraying and water bombing hours. In the contract we specified the requirement for a fixed wing pilot was a minimum of 1,000 hours low level spraying time. We took off and I immediately questioned his experience. His aim seemed to be to try and make me sick with his steep turns and quick descents and climbs. I waited for him to get tired of this demonstration since we had 10 or so flying hours to do that day, which he eventually did. He managed to frighten me with his spraying. An experienced crop spraying pilot will always attempt to fly into wind to get more lift, with the sun behind him. Once he has released his load he will always climb sufficiently to execute a turn and only descend when he is positioned for the next spray release. With Ian we were turning round trees and we were so low that once or twice he lost sight of the river! By the end of the day he was worn out ... and I didn't feel much better with the anxiety. We landed on a rough airstrip in Ghana and booked into an African hotel for the night. At dinner we discussed his flying when I told him that I did not think he would last too long and I mentioned to him some of the tricks I had learned in my spraying experience.

I mentioned my concerns to the then Project manager of the aerial contractor. With the forthcoming larvicide release demonstration for the donors I requested that the other more experienced fixed wing pilot should fly the aeroplane but he insisted that Ian would be quite capable and it would shatter his confidence if we didn't allow him. He was a very weak Project Manager, and even he was soon to be replaced.

The Wayen accident

For the demonstration I arranged for the chief helicopter pilot Bill to make a helicopter flight first, to keep well away from the crowd, to come to the hover at a minimum distance from the bridge of 100 metres for the release and make sure the spray did not come near the crowd, carefully checking the wind drift first.

He was a careful and very competent pilot and did exactly as he was requested. I had a hand held radio set and I then called Ian, who was nearby in the fixed wing to come and demonstrate his release of larvicide. As with the helicopter, I had given him instructions of what was required. I had told him to fly across the flow of the river west to east 200 metres well south of the crowd on the bridge and release larvicide as he crossed (into wind) and that we did not want a flying exhibition and not to go above or near the onlookers! I was standing on the bridge parapet higher above the crowd and holding the

B Cliff with the hand-held radio to contact the pilots

172

microphone of the radio in my hand. There were a number of villagers from Wayen and with all the donors there must have been 200-300 people watching the demonstration. As he approached I asked Ian to do a dummy run first but he commented that it was not necessary! He came in from the south and descended on to the river with his wheels virtually on the surface and to my disgust flew up river towards the crowd and the bridge. I was tempted to call him on the radio but thought it would confuse him so I kept silent. I had also warned him about 10 wires that followed the road and crossed the bridge just below the parapet. People were so alarmed that many were flat on the ground as he approached. He dropped the larvicide only a few metres from us at about 2 metres altitude and then climbed over the crowd and bridge *into* all the wires which were immediately cut and they all fell into the crowd. In spite of towing part of the fractured pole and wires he managed to keep airborne and climb away remarking to me on the radio that he thought he had hit the wires! Which of course I confirmed and warned him he was towing part of the pole. People ran to me to tell me that there were some injuries. Looking at three African boys standing next to me I saw something on the ground and picked it up. To my horror it was a boy's cap with his scalp in it with the poor boy looking at me wide-eyed and not aware of what was going on, one other boy was holding his right arm which had been broken with both the radius and ulna exposed in a fractured state. Since I was standing on the bridge parapet and above everyone else, had the fractured wires fallen one metre nearer to me I would probably have been decapitated!

Carrying the boy's cap and scalp and with the help of the Canadian representative, a doctor as she soon announced, I put the two boys in my vehicle and drove to the hospital at Ouagadougou. It was midday with a number of staff just leaving for their lunch break. The surgeon whom I knew was amongst them and I stopped him and told him what had taken place. He immediately turned round and asked me to follow with the two boys. The Canadian lady followed immediately announcing that she was a doctor and wanted to come in. She clearly upset the surgeon and he turned to me and said, "Barry, get rid of this woman", to which I then obliged. The surgeon immediately operated and sewed the scalp back on, telling me he doubted it would "take". He also put the boy's arm in plaster and asked me to keep in contact with him. I then went to see the Programme Director, a fine man from Haiti. He had already heard about the accident and was very upset. His first reaction was to tell me that as Chief of Aerial operations and in charge of the demonstration I should have made certain that an accident in front of the donors could never occur and his feelings were to "fire" me. I felt devastated but, once he knew the circumstances he later relented and kept me on!

Apart from the Wayen debacle there were two other accidents involving our aircraft. The fixed wing aircraft, then a Pilatus Porter came to grief whilst treating the Comoe river. Both the pilot and my colleague Jeff Henderickx were uninjured and very lucky to survive for the aircraft was a complete write-off. I had a radio in my office as did the company project manager

*Both the pilot and my colleague Jeff
Henderickx survived this accident whilst
treating the Comoe River*

and we kept in touch with all the aircraft when they were away from base on treatment flights.

The pilots were asked to report when they landed at a fuel cache and which river they were treating, so we knew roughly where they were at all times. A Canadian helicopter pilot Larry made a radio message to me that he was landing at a particular fuel cache to refuel and would then be treating a certain river in Ivory Coast. There was no further radio call that day and the company Project manager and myself became concerned with a lack of response to our repeated attempts to call him. We undertook a helicopter flight over the river he had reported and found Larry's helicopter, apparently burned out

175

and landed on a sand bank mid-river in a gorge. We had some difficulty getting into the gorge where we found Larry still at the controls, strapped to his seat and burned to death. With scorched trees on his approach it seemed that the helicopter had caught fire in flight and he had immediately landed it where the lack of forward speed the fire engulfed him and the machine. We evacuated the body and we were in the awful position of having to inform his mother in Canada that he had lost his life. She insisted that we arranged to have his body repatriated but we soon came across all the hierarchy involved. A lead-lined casket with various chemicals installed is required, almost impossible to arrange in the wilds of Africa and his mother eventually gave us her permission to inter his body with a simple service at a local African village cemetary. Larry was a very experienced pilot/engineer and it was a terrible loss to his family and the River Blindness programme.

Adventures in aviation ended for me when I resigned from the River Blindness programme in order to return to England to assist my sister with my elderly ailing parents.

It was a fitting end to aviation adventures when I left the Programme in 1986.

Chapter 11

Sailing Adventures

National Service

I regarded it as fortunate that I was a young man of eligible age when National Service in the armed forces was obligatory after the Second World War. Attending the required interviews in Leeds aged 18, I was asked which service I preferred. On replying, "the Royal Navy", I was abruptly told that there were no vacancies in the Navy for two-year conscripts, and that I should choose a branch of the Army. Without much idea of what might be suitable, I agreed to the interviewing officer's suggestion that the paratroopers would be an interesting alternative.

It was therefore a surprise, and a relief to my mother when instructions arrived to report to the Royal Navy at Portsmouth barracks. Living with other men from all walks of life was a fascinating experience and I coped easily with the serious discipline and really enjoyed the fine camaraderie. After a period of basic training at the barracks, I was given a brief posting to a small mine-laying ship, to which I was instructed to report early one morning as it would be leaving for sea that same day. My kit-bag and hammock were thrown down an open hatch and I was told to follow. It led to a small mess deck where some of the ship's crew were assembled, sitting on wooden benches. Immediately my legs appeared down the steel ladder, a heavily-bearded sailor sitting in a corner exclaimed, "Ah, look what the Admiral has sent us!" As I later learned, he was a man who commanded much respect, for he was one of the only three survivors from the sinking of H.M.S. *Hood*.

My time on the ship was very short and soon after a voyage to Ireland I was given a "shore" posting to the torpedo school, H.M.S. *Vernon* in Portsmouth. The shore station had numerous yachts; "Victory" class boats were available (the boats were half-decked and, with a long keel, they were ideal for weekend forays to sea). I took full advantage of the chance to learn how to sail. Being engineless, they were also ideal for learning how to handle tides and cope with the difficult entrance to Portsmouth Harbour under sail. There was only limited interest among my other shipmates so I soon contacted Jim Rennie, my earlier climbing companion who by then was doing National Service in the army and stationed not far from Portsmouth. We had some fine weekends together sailing to the Isle of Wight and its harbours, cooking and sleeping on the boat in some interesting anchorages.

Entry and exit from Portsmouth Harbour under sail with so much other shipping about was always a nervous and challenging experience. At one attempt to get out of the harbour entrance we had a serious encounter with the Portsmouth-Gosport ferry which at that time was operated by two sea-bed chains which the ferry picked up and with them pulled itself along. On a windless day and using only the tide for movement, we got on a collision course with the ferry rapidly approaching and the chains surfacing beneath us. A megaphone shout from the ferry captain suggesting, "Why don't you wrap up?!" made us paddle away with a small paddle we had.

On completion of National Service in the Navy, there was no further opportunity for sailing for some time but I joined the Royal Naval Sailing Association, which enabled me to charter Royal Naval yachts, kept and maintained by the Association. Once I was fit enough and recovered from the aircraft accident, I chartered a yacht from the Association, a 30-foot sloop named *Annette* berthed at Whale Island in Portsmouth harbour. I invited Michael Robinson to join me for a week's sailing, which he readily accepted while asking if it would be in order for his girlfriend, Tessa, to come along. I agreed and the two came down to Portsmouth to assist in taking delivery of the yacht. The Petty Officer in charge immediately informed me that the previous charterer had managed to damage the engine, which had therefore been taken out for repair. He said that he would allow us to take the boat for a one-week charter without the engine, if we were happy to accept it. After discussing the implications with Michael and Tessa I agreed and we duly tackled the exit from Portsmouth Harbour under sail alone.

With a good wind we sailed out and exited the Solent by way of the Needles to the west of the Isle of Wight. That evening, whilst attempting to get into Swanage Bay to anchor for the night, the wind dropped completely and we became becalmed. We drifted back and forth with the tide and current some distance off the Swanage cliffs. All we could do was sit and wait for wind and since there were three of us, I suggested that the night be divided into three watches, with the person on watch simply to sit in the cockpit and keep a lookout, calling me if the situation deteriorated.

To my surprise, after taking the first watch myself, Michael asked if he and Tessa could stand their watches together when they would offer to keep a lookout for the rest of the night. I therefore descended into the cabin for a good night's sleep. I could hear a low buzz of conversation as the night progressed and periodically asking if all was well, I was told to keep sleeping! As dawn broke I ventured on deck to be told that they had some news for me; during the night they had become engaged to be married! With a fresh wind starting to blow we sailed easily into Swanage Bay and anchored. Being a Sunday morning it was suggested that, "as Captain" it would be an act of chivalry to row ashore alone in the dinghy we had, to get the Sunday paper! I duly complied and on my return we had more sailing, successfully returning the boat under sail to the Navy base in Portsmouth Harbour. I was duly invited to the wedding.

Sunstream

Eventually, I bought my own boat. It was a 33-foot sloop – a "Windfall" boat. (Sometime after the end of the 1939-45 war, a number of German yachts were commandeered by the Royal Navy and sailed across from German harbours to Britain, to be used by the armed forces. These were called "Windfall" yachts and were all very fine German-built boats.) *Sunstream*, the boat I bought, was such a craft and was first allocated to the army and kept in Scotland. A Royal Navy Lieutenant-Commander bought it from the army and used it for his personal enjoyment, eventually putting it up for sale where I spotted it in the Royal Naval Association journal. I bought it from him in Greenock where it was then berthed. It was my intention to sail the boat to Mombasa in East Africa and it was hence necessary to first sail down the Irish Sea to Falmouth in Cornwall where I had an offer of summer employment with a company operating flights from Land's End airport.

Once again, for crew I contacted Michael Robinson, then happily married and living in

Sunstream. The "Windfall" boat in Caernarfon Bay

Inverness in Scotland. He travelled down to Greenock with Tessa and we prepared the boat for sea. Down the Firth of Clyde we experienced a strong wind and looking up at the mast to check the rigging, I suddenly saw a longitudinal split occur on a seam, running down the mast from the spreaders to the deck. We immediately shortened sail and made our way into Dunoon where I knew my climbing mate Rusty was working for the Benmore Adventure Centre. Beckoning to a fisherman, also anchoring his boat, I asked where good

183

holding ground was and he indicated closer inshore, which is where we let go the anchor. All three of us were wet through and tired, so we retired to rest.

Within an hour there was a crunching noise and hurriedly reaching the cockpit, I soon realised that we were hard aground. Michael's first reaction was to insist that Tessa put on a life jacket, which she rapidly did while I indicated that all she had to do was step over the side and walk ashore (*Sunstream* drew 2½ feet)! Once ashore myself, I walked to the Adventure Centre to find Rusty who came down to help us de-mast the boat. A local boat builder offered to glue the seam on the mast and band it with glass-fibre. Two days later, and suitably repaired, we put to sea again and cruised to Lamlash on the Isle of Arran for water and petrol before venturing into the Irish Sea.

We entered the North Channel between Scotland and Ireland at nightfall and with a faltering engine and little wind were buffeted about for a number of hours. *Sunstream* had a two-cylinder Stewart Turner petrol engine and I soon realised that it was not in good order and was consuming considerable quantities of engine oil. In fact we ran out of oil and I decided to shut it down before it seized. With a dying wind we had little steerage way. There was indeed an awful racket coming from slapping sails and loose rigging; so much so that Michael, resting down below, suddenly requested that as his wife was unable to sleep because of the noise, I should do something about it. I had to abruptly remind him that we were on a sailing ship and noise is to be expected and tolerated.

As morning lightened and a promise of a better wind we were some miles to the east of the Isle of Man, witnessing a beautiful sunrise and a calm sea. Spirits became much better as we breakfasted in the cockpit. A large tanker appeared on the horizon on a reciprocal course to us and as it came alongside about half a mile distant, I was somewhat alarmed when Michael, ever conscious of his wife's well-being, grabbed my bright red duvet jacket and stood on the foredeck waving it at the tanker. Asked what he was doing, he replied, "Maybe they can let us have some oil." I requested him to step down immediately as the tanker, with a man on the bridge glaring down at us through binoculars thundered on its way, understandably without any acknowledgement or friendly wave.

We had a very pleasant sail down the Irish Sea which made me realise what a wonderful boat I had bought. Being narrow beamed and low in the water, it was, however, rather a wet boat to sail in a heavy sea and I thought perhaps not the right type of yacht to sail to Mombasa in Kenya.

In the afternoon we were abeam Anglesey and sailing down the Caernarfon coast, when Michael came up with another bombshell: "Since Tessa had such a bad night's sleep ... we need to go ashore to spend the night in a hotel." Spying the coastline, he suggested going into a very rocky cove we could see some way off. Words were exchanged and I refused to sail into a rocky cove without an engine, having just spent half my life's savings buying *Sunstream*. Tessa appeared completely unflappable to me and seemed to be enjoying the adventure. We rounded the south-west point of Caernarfon and left Bardsey Island to starboard. Aberdaron Bay soon came into view with Aberdaron village and a prominent large white building, which Michael immediately pronounced as a suitable hotel! As evening approached we anchored in the bay and Michael and Tessa took off in the dinghy for "a good night's rest." With a rising wind and changing the anchorage, I had anything but the same, but I did enjoy the challenge of handling the boat alone under sail and re-setting the anchor.

In the morning a refreshed crew returned for a good sail across Cardigan Bay. Then another bombshell: "We need to go into Milford Haven for me to get back to work in Inverness." Michael seemed exhausted to me and he went below deck and into a deep sleep. Tessa, now somewhat more confident and at ease, ably assisted sailing the yacht into Milford Haven and we had anchored amongst some tankers before Michael appeared on deck, surprised at our accomplishment. They duly departed and I was left alone to contemplate the next step.

I telephoned a pilot friend of mine, Chris, who readily agreed to join me for the sail around Land's End to Falmouth. He soon appeared on the jetty and I rowed the dinghy in to pick him up. The dinghy was an empty shell of fibreglass with one thwart and only about three inches of draft. Being so light it was a dangerous craft from which to embark and disembark. Once on the jetty myself, I instructed Chris how to get in by placing one foot in the centre of the boat. As he did so, he stepped straight on the gunwale and in a split second the dinghy inverted on top of him. Soaked through, he climbed up the nearby jetty steps where we both collapsed with laughter. I hunted for a third crew member and Ade, a keen sailor and friend working for the BBC, agreed to join us. The three of us sailed the boat across the mouth of the Bristol Channel to Newquay, where Chris then contacted his employer to find that he was required back for his flying duties. He had been a good shipmate and I was sorry he was unable to stay longer. Ade and I then sailed the boat around Land's End and with a strong westerly wind we set the parachute spinnaker (a spinnaker with a hole in the centre) to arrive off the Lizard doing about seven knots. A delightful cruise into Falmouth Bay followed, then tricky sailing into the Helford River where I moored the boat for the summer, whilst engaged in flying at Land's End airport with a de Havilland Rapide aeroplane.

Living on and returning to the yacht each evening was delightful; the dreadful dinghy always providing a challenge to get out to the yacht, moored as it was in mid-river. By November the work diminished and the weather deteriorated. One night and rowing out to the yacht in a westerly gale I had difficulty making way in the strong crosswind. With its high freeboard and shallow draft the wind had more effect upon the dinghy than the oars! By going some way up river I managed to be blown down onto *Sunstream*. Relieved to be

187

safely on board, I made the dinghy fast to the usual cleat on the stern of the yacht and went below. As I went down the companionway steps I heard a noise and looking round, saw that the cleat had parted from the yacht with the dinghy caught by the gale, already twenty feet away and rapidly heading out to sea and the river mouth. I immediately stripped off and dived after it into the icy river. Once with the dinghy, progress back up the river to the yacht proved impossible, as I drifted out with it, before checking progress out to sea by swimming diagonally to the current and eventually reaching shallow water on the north bank. Naked, and with hypothermia rapidly taking hold I considered the position I was in. Reluctant to seek help in the state I was in, I decided to attempt swimming upstream in the shallow water beside the bank, pushing the dinghy in front of me and by doing this managed to get some distance up river beyond the yacht. Judging the right moment, and stemming wind and tide, I managed to get the dinghy back to *Sunstream* where I had only just enough strength left to get myself out of the water. Hours later I stopped shivering and slowly recovered.

With the offer of immediate employment in Guyana and a reluctance to sell the yacht, I sailed *Sunstream* into Falmouth and arranged for it to be laid up at Falmouth Boat Construction Company. It remained there for a considerable time but, with no possibility of sailing in the foreseeable future, it seemed pointless to continue ownership. The boat company arranged a sale and I never saw the yacht again.

I later owned a small 18-foot boat in Mombasa Harbour for a while when I flew for Air Kenya out of Mombasa, but my next boat was a much more serious venture.

Batian

I retired from The World Health Organisation in 1987 and returned to the U.K., principally to help with my ailing elderly parents. After the death of my father, I searched for an ocean-going boat. Initially a wooden 40-foot ketch for sale in Portugal seemed suitable, but after two visits there, a survey showed sufficient rot to cause me to withdraw from proceeding further. I then learned of a 36-foot ketch for sale in Greece and since it was about to be sailed back to the U.K., I hurriedly flew down there to take a look as it was out of the water, enabling me to inspect the hull. An Australian delivery crew of man and wife were on board. As friends of the owner, they had some cruising experi-ence on the boat and considered it an excellent craft. I knew

Batian out of the water in Corsica for anti-fouling

189

of the reputation of Colin Archer boats, and this was a genuine one, built of mahogany and oak in 1962 in Risor, Norway. (Colin Archer – half English, half Norwegian – lived at the turn of the last century in Norway, and designed rescue boats there, as well as the famous FRAM – Arctic and Antarctic voyages with Amundsen and Nansen). Casually looking at it, I felt there was too much work to be done on it and I turned it down.

I stayed at a small guesthouse near to the yard where the yacht was berthed and helped the Australians prepare the craft for the voyage to the U.K. I became friendly with them and eventually they asked if I would like to sail with them for some of the voyage. Since I had no immediate other plans I agreed and we headed for the Corinth Canal. As an ex-Royal Australian Air Force navigator, Pat was a competent sailor and clearly passionate and very knowledgeable about wooden boats. Both he and his wife Judith were delightful to be with and together we overcame the various problems we encountered, particularly with a temperamental diesel engine that kept failing at awkward moments. I slowly became quite attached to the yacht and with Pat's enthusiasm, realised that it probably was very suitable for me.

After the Corinth Canal we sailed south of Sicily into Cagliari in the south of Sardinia. I left the boat there in order to travel back to the U.K. to negotiate with the owner, whilst Pat and Judith continued to Gibraltar. Once the sale had materialised I took delivery of it in Gibraltar with Pat helping me prepare for a return to the Mediterranean. At that time I had aspirations to live in Corsica, an island I had previously visited and with its mountains and attractive sea I felt it would offer an ideal life style to suit my passions. For the voyage to Corsica I recruited Tim, a man with whom I had sailed, with eighteen others, delivering the Whitbread yacht *Great Britain II* from Plymouth to Tenerife two years previously. We were somewhat "shorthanded" with just the two of us and so we sailed cautiously, first to Cartagena in southern Spain, then Minorca and a land-fall eventually in Corsica at Propriano on the south-west coast; there Tim had to leave to return to his work in the U.K. From Propriano to Porto-Vecchio on the southeast coast, Corsican friends Stephano and Isabelle helped sail the boat through the Straits of Bonifacio, between

Batian anchored in Porto Novo Bay, Corsica

Corsica and Sardinia, to Porto-Vecchio where I arranged for a permanent mooring for the yacht.

During the early years of my retirement, in between searching for, and eventually buying a house in the Yorkshire Dales, I spent eight months of each year in Corsica, living on the yacht. Slowly I made numerous modifications to the boat and prepared it for serious ocean voyaging. I renewed all the standing and running rigging, and fitted new sails including storm sails and ordered an orange tri-sail, anticipating encountering heavy seas. It was absorbing and fascinating work which I really enjoyed and on registering the yacht with British Shipping I named it *Batian*, the highest peak of Mt Kenya, as a fitting mark of the reverence I have for that lovely mountain. With 1¼" mahogany planking, double frames of oak and a triple oak frame supporting the main mast, the boat weighed fourteen tons and was solid and stable enough for such a fitting name.

Chapter 12

The Atlantic

To South America …

Whilst flying the Beaver float plane in Guyana, with a base on the Demerara River, I had always intended that one day I would sail a boat across the Atlantic and make a landfall up the Demerara. Indeed, at that time, I already possessed the sea chart of the approaches to Georgetown, the capital of Guyana.

When *Batian* was ready for such a voyage, I recruited, yet again, Michael Robinson (then divorced) and, once more, Tim who, having crossed the Atlantic in the Whitbread yacht *Great Britain II* (72 feet), wished to sail across in a "much smaller boat" such as *Batian* (36 feet). We sailed from Corsica to Cartagena in southern Spain. There, Michael returned to the U.K. and Tim and I continued to Gibraltar. It was my intention to navigate across the Atlantic by sextant alone, using the sun, moon and stars and in spite of some criticism, I shunned the use of satellite navigation (which eventually became G.P.S.). Indeed the previous owner of the boat, a surgeon from Warwickshire, with whom I corresponded, considered it "irresponsible" not to have a back-up navigation system to sextant only. I enjoyed and was passionate about celestial navigation, however, and quite confident in my ability hence scorning other modern aids.

Arriving safely in Gibraltar, very satisfied with the performance of the boat thus far, Tim and I felt it would make for a much easier passage to have a third crew member. In Gibraltar at that time there was (and probably still is) a local newsagent which exhibited advertisements of crew looking for trans-Atlantic passages. I scanned the shop window and a particular notice caused me to make contact with the advertiser. A single, middle-aged lady from Guernsey who had recently sold her shop in Dukesa, southern Spain, had a yearning to cross the Atlantic on a small yacht. Tim was more attracted to another advert by two teenaged Danish girls! Not too sure what criteria Tim had in mind, I decided to interview the Guernsey lady.

She arrived at the jetty where *Batian* was berthed and immediately impressed me. Quiet and unassuming, she did not have much sailing experience but with a background of running a B&B establishment she described herself as a very capable chef and was clearly passionate about the sea. I suggested she help provision the yacht and to accompany us on a trial basis, initially to Portugal where we intended to call in to see Pat and Judith (the Australians), who were

Sheila and Michael Robinson at dinner in Batian's saloon

196

resident there on their own yacht. There, we would review together whether she would continue into the Atlantic. Her name was Sheila and, without Tim, who had to make a quick visit to the U.K. to arrange and collect Guyana visas, she and I provisioned *Batian* for a proposed three-week voyage. Once Tim had returned with the necessary visas, we cast off and headed to sea.

When darkness fell we confronted a westerly gale and with seas breaking over the foredeck, I suggested that Sheila and Tim could leave me alone in the cockpit where I was already on the helm and wet through and go below to keep dry and warm. Movement of the boat was violent and they readily agreed; I felt somewhat queasy myself and imagined both of them to be very unwell down below. How wrong I was! After an hour the hatch suddenly opened and Sheila's smiling face indicated that she was enjoying it and she asked if I would "like a cup of tea". She also informed me that Tim was not feeling too good. The tea brought some life back into me and made me realise what a gem we had taken on in Sheila. She was never seasick and moved about on a heaving boat like a real professional. Nothing fazed her and at Portugal she expressed her confidence in my handling of the yacht and was very anxious to be allowed to continue. Tim and I were very pleased and honoured. The eagle eye of Pat in Portugal, as a hardened sailor with experience of selecting crew, also confirmed my feelings and he came down to the jetty to wish us "bon voyage". He stood forlorn; clearly he would have liked to be with us. I was aware that he was ill and suffering, but I never saw him again for he died soon after seeing us off. Sadly, I was unaware of his death until we called in to see him again on our return nine months later.

We had a good passage to Tenerife where we berthed in the northern yacht basin. Just before dusk we were asked to move ahead as a powerboat would be coming in and would need that berth when it arrived. Tim recognised the man on deck as Robert Maxwell! He vacated the berth before us the following morning. We left later as we had first to pick up some sea charts in the town. We had a small radio on board and on leaving the port, heard on the BBC news that Maxwell had gone missing from his boat at sea off Tenerife and we had probably sailed through that very area!

We set a course for the Cape Verde islands and with good winds took eight days to reach them. On the final day visibility deteriorated and we had some difficulty in picking up the light on Santo Antão island. Our navigation had been accurate, using Venus, Sirius, Capella and the sun with the sextant, and the course took us directly between Santo Antão and São Vincente. We sailed into Mindelo on São Vincente where we stayed for a few days.

Our next leg was to be across the Atlantic to South America with a landfall in Georgetown, Guyana. A few hours after we left the Cape Verde islands, in what appeared to be fairly light winds, Tim and I set the large light cruising chute. It was a rash decision on my part and with *Batian* rolling heavily in an

Atlantic swell the chute immediately ripped across the centre and we had an anxious time trying to avoid the remains becoming entangled round the mainmast head. We got it down safely eventually, and somewhat chastened and determined to be more prudent, we continued with a reefed mainsail. We used the mizzen sail occasionally until I noticed that I was having to adjust and tighten the shroud rigging stays very frequently. The mizzen mast appeared to be descending and an examination beneath the cockpit confirmed that indeed it was! The main oak beam supporting the mast had split and was bending under the weight of the mast, particularly with a sail set. As a consequence, we were unable to use the mizzen sail again for the rest of our voyage to Georgetown.

With the prospect of two to three weeks at sea we tried to adopt an easy routine. By day we relaxed, sharing the helm between us. At night, however, we worked two-hour watches with the three aboard hence then each having four hours off. Sheila made the evening meal which we ate between 18.00 and 20.00 and, during that time, I

The Aries wind vane steering the boat - Tim on watch

199

took and worked out star sights. Tim then took the 20.00-22.00 watch, to be relieved by me at 22.00 for the 22.00-24.00 watch. Sheila requested, and appeared to prefer, the 00.00-02.00, (a situation I later regretted as she became very tired and I failed to recognise her fatigue). Tim then relieved her at 02.00 and I came on again for 04.00-06.00 in order to identify and take star shots at dawn. With an Aries wind vane to hold the ship's course, there was little to do apart from keeping a sharp look-out and adjusting the wind vane from time to time. If any lights were sighted I requested to be called to identify them; similarly for any sail changes, which were done by Tim and I. To avoid disruption at night, however, we usually shortened sail before dusk and left the rig so until dawn. The aim was for us all to enjoy the sail and challenge across to South America without any stress and, I believe, we managed that. We caught fish (pictured) and frequently feasted on Sheila's excellent fish pies.

In spite of being in the N.E. trade winds, and at a tropical latitude, we did not have particularly good weather; we experienced quite a lot of rain and poor visibility. After eighteen days at sea, and a few days before our landfall at Georgetown, at dawn in rain and mist, a very large ship appeared on our stern. Since we had had no horizon or sights for a few days, I attempted to call the ship on our V.H.F. radio for a position check. For some time there was no response, but eventually, as the ship came on our starboard beam at about ½ mile distance, a very Scottish voice asked who was calling. I described *Batian* as a small yacht on his port beam. We only had a small, white storm jib flying and, surrounded by white-capped breaking seas, he was unable to see us, not even on his radar. To identify himself to us he said he was "very large", and if "410,000 tons" meant anything to us. I replied that indeed it did, and he then gave me the ship's name, the *Star Queen,* which he said was one of the world's largest tankers, inbound to the Gulf of Mexico from the Arabian Gulf and carrying oil. He gave us his position and indeed, it was within ½ mile of our own calculated one. He queried, "Why on earth are you going to Guyana?" and said he had "only been there once and didn't want to go again!" He wished us "bon voyage" and disappeared into the mist. Both Sheila and Tim commented on how nice it was to hear another human voice and they both seemed relieved that "we knew where we were!"

Georgetown, Guyana – again

As mentioned earlier, I already possessed the sea chart of the approaches to Georgetown in Guyana from when I used to fly the Beaver floatplane there some twenty years previously. We now had this very chart on board and, although it was well out of date and even then, marked "unfit for navigation", I used it as we approached land. Some thirty miles off the coast the so-called "landfall" buoy was marked on the chart. After numerous evening and morning star shots with the sextant to pinpoint our position, I plotted a course to the landfall buoy, carefully marked on the chart with latitude and longitude. We could not find it and I had a very anxious time checking and re-checking my workings with the heavenly bodies. (I have our old log book in front of me as I write, and

I note that at 06.30 we used Pollux, Arcturus, Sirius and Venus to calculate our position – at North 7° 13' , West 57° 35' .)

Towards evening a ship appeared on the horizon and on an identical course to us; I assumed it was heading into Georgetown and Demerara River as we were. It

Navigating by sextant

202

closed and overtook us some distance away. With failing light and wind we started the engine and held our course. Visibility was very poor but we thought we could see the loom of light ahead. In complete blackness we suddenly found ourselves amongst numerous twelve-foot wooden canoes, all unlit and with a single person aboard. No one spoke, and I felt we were about to be boarded and raided. Sheila was terrified and I asked her to go below and remain out of sight. I also asked Tim to go below and read the depth sounder. He reported that we had six feet of water under the keel! I immediately "did a 180°" and took a reciprocal course back out to sea.

We then found that we were amongst a number of vertical wooden poles, presumably fish traps. We cleared these and continued out to sea until dawn. We had a V.H.F. radio on board and, soon after dawn, on Channel 16 – the emergency channel – I heard traffic calling "Georgetown lighthouse". I called them myself and reported that we were on the approach to Georgetown, between the landfall buoy and the Demerara River mouth. I was curtly told that the landfall buoy had been removed some thirty years ago(!), and was requested to report what ship we were and our tonnage! When I replied, "fourteen tons and a yacht", there was stunned silence, followed by the news that no yacht had been there for a number of years. We were then asked if we had custom clearance and a pre-arranged agent to deal with our entry. A confused conversation followed, and eventual permission granted to enter, with a proposed agent allocated to us. I was also informed that Georgetown was not a safe place to berth – a few days previously a tanker, anchored in mid-river, had been boarded, the captain held at gunpoint and the ship ransacked! Later, the top of the lighthouse came into view as we made our way into the mouth of the Demerara River with myself, Sheila and Tim feeling very uneasy. We berthed onto a wooden jetty with "our agent" coming aboard and demanding a huge fee in U.S. dollars! My experience in dealing with such situations in Africa suddenly became very useful and with calm diplomacy, an unpleasant confrontation was averted. Indeed, the agent became very friendly and even accepted a cup of tea! We were

then advised that if the yacht was left where we were presently berthed, whether we were on board or not, we would "lose everything to robbers". In a phone call to the military, the agent managed to get permission for us to go up river and berth at their jetty, which he felt would be much safer. Tired as we were with Sheila visibly shaking, we moved upstream to the

Batian in the Demerara River, tied to the wreck

Guyana Defence Force jetty and tied up alongside a wreck of a boat. I made contact with the commanding officer, who allowed us to use their showers and agree to a fee in U.S. dollars for the berth. As with the agent, he also became very friendly and helpful. We had been at sea for twenty days!

The Demerara River is tidal at its mouth and is dirty brown in colour, with all the detritus from the town coming down on the current and tide. It cannot be described as pleasant to witness and coupled with all this, the single manned canoes came down each evening, heading out to sea to fish; these were the ones we had confronted on our arrival off the coast at night. Much to Sheila's concern, some of them would hang on to our bulwarks as they drifted past and would "eye us up" (her words). Tim only went ashore once, in order to get a flight back to the U.K., and very soon left.

Remembering how I used to live in and enjoy Georgetown when I was bush flying there with the Beaver, I always felt safe and at ease, for I was the life-line of many of the – somewhat doubtful – characters I knew who made their living diving for gold and diamonds in the interior. With those memories in mind, I casually took a taxi and went into town to get some spares we needed for *Batian*. When the taxi driver advised me to keep the door locked on my side, I should have expected action of some sort, but I was not ready for it when it did arrive. We drove into an area known as Tiger Bay, where the taxi driver accompanied me into a store. I knew the area for it was where I used to play water polo for Guyana in the swimming pool nearly twenty years previously. I noticed that the girl cashier on the desk was enclosed in a metal cage which should have also set alarms going. I made the required purchases, paid and stepped outside with the driver. I was immediately jumped on by three men and thrown face down to the ground. The rucksack was snatched from my back and my watch ripped off my wrist within seconds, with the driver sensibly stepping back; with their spoil, the three men scarpered. The driver suggested going to the police immediately which we then did. He described what had taken place, and when he mentioned Tiger Bay, the sergeant said, "What, you took this white man into Tiger Bay? We [the police] don't go in there!" The driver got a severe dressing-down and, of course, my money, watch, parts and rucksack were lost forever. I felt fortunate to be relatively unscathed, apart from a few bruises. Back at the boat, and telling Sheila what had taken place, I got a further reprimand. Understandably she was very upset, and reminded me that I had promised her blue seas and coconut trees in a tropical paradise and all I had come up with was a filthy river, fear and violence, and a nightly visit by a rat from the wreck alongside didn't help matters! She refused to step ashore!

Further misfortune was to follow. In stepping off *Batian* onto the boat wreck, I slipped on the metal deck and twisted my knee. Walking and even standing was painful and, being now short-handed without Tim, I felt we should delay sailing to Trinidad as we had planned until I was fit enough. That resulted in a prolonged stay at the Guyanan Defence Force berth, which meant Christmas and New Year in the Demerara River!

We invited the Commander-in-Chief of the base, Lieutenant Earl Daniels and his wife to come and have Christmas dinner on board. He readily and enthusiastically accepted. We asked him to arrive at 12.30 and Sheila accordingly cooked a magnificent meal. By 13.30, with still no sign of Lt Daniels and his wife we did what justice we could to the meal. At 15.00 Lt Daniels turned up, not with his wife but with two girl friends. As we diplomatically pointed out the time, he said, "Ah, that is the trouble with you English – you are obsessed with time." He went on further; "In my training, I spent one year with the Royal Navy at Plymouth learning navigating. What I remember about the town is that everywhere you look there are clocks. You let time run your lives. You should learn to relax like the Guyanese, and not be so serious." He and his girlfriends were delightful company and they were perfectly content with tea and biscuits, since the rest of the meal by then was ruined. I then asked how he had enjoyed the navigating course and using a sextant. "It was very difficult", he said, and "I couldn't get the hang of it. In calculating the position at sea on a Royal Naval ship, my calculations put us in the middle of France and I failed the course."

At New Year's Eve we were advised that the base would be celebrating with alcohol flowing freely. I could well imagine what that would be like and since the ratings were all aware that Sheila was on board, she agreed to be locked away in the forward cabin. There was a lot of noise and gunshots and we were both relieved at dawn on New Year's Day to be still unscathed!

I was fit again to sail in January and out of interest I asked Lt Daniels how he navigated to Trinidad. "Ah," he said, "take a course to the north out of the Demerara River, give it half a hour, then make a left and follow the coast until you see Trinidad"! We left early in the New Year and had a good passage to Trinidad, where we found another delightful Caribbean man on the Customs jetty. "Have you any guns on board?" he asked. "No," I replied." "Tanks?" he said. "No, no tanks," I replied. "Tanks," again, he said, before I realised he meant "thanks" – the Caribbean way!

There, Sheila enjoyed the warm blue sea and the coconut trees, before she left to return by air to England.

Repair and return across the Atlantic

Ashore in Trinidad I replaced the oak beam beneath the mizzen mast and prepared the yacht for the voyage back across the Atlantic. Once again the problem of finding suitable crew arose. I contacted David Clarke, a climbing companion from Leeds University days who had wanted to come on the outward voyage but who had been unable to accept then, due to his father's failing health. Now, with the death of his father, he was ready for part of the return sail. It was my intention to take a great circle route to the Azores, sailing abeam and to the east of Bermuda. Dave had been a member of Bonington's south face of Everest expedition, climbing up to Camp 4 as equipment officer and a valuable member of the team. To my surprise I received a letter from Sheila, asking if she could return and join us for the voyage home, to which I readily agreed. I was aware that Dave was quite a heavy drinker and smoker which worried me. Out of respect for Sheila and myself, as well as the safety of the ship, I asked him if he could possibly live without cigarettes and alcohol, to which he readily agreed.

He duly appeared and, with Sheila aboard, we set our northerly course. Within a day we developed a problem with the alternator, and we had to put into Tobago – Man o' War Bay – to attempt to repair it. We managed to get it working again and once more returned to sea. It failed again so we called in to Barbados to look for a replacement.

Batian at the quay in Barbados for a new alternator

Ready for sea again, we left under full sail with the steady north-east trade winds and, apart from periodically putting a reef in main and mizzen, we kept full sail up for almost a week. We got into a good routine, working similar watches to our outward passage, with everyone religiously writing up the log at every two-hour watch change and all happy and enjoying themselves working the ship. Dave soon proved to be excellent at rope work, as to be expected from a mountaineer and he became very adept at reefing and shaking reefs out single-handedly, leaving me free to enjoy the navigating. As we worked our way northwards, we experienced some rain and wind change. It took thirteen days to get to a latitude abeam Bermuda where we witnessed a build-up of a bank of cloud to the west early one morning. Sure enough, we had run into the westerlies, and with wind now on the port quarter we were able to tack and alter course to 040° to continue our great circle route to the Azores. That evening, with a perfect horizon and clear sky at 19.00, I was able to accurately fix our position in mid-Atlantic at North 32° 12', West 50° 10', using Jupiter and six stars: Kochab, Vega, Antares, Spica, Regulus and Dubhe.

Trade wind sailing now altered drastically and we soon ran into heavy weather. A Force 8 gale came two days later, making us shorten sail to our orange storm trysail and white storm jib. We all handled the storm well and the boat behaved magnificently. Weighing fourteen tons and solidly built, *Batian* was not a fast boat but it was built for heavy weather and not once did we doubt its splendid pedigree as a Colin Archer.

Above: Batian's saloon. Left to right are Dave Clarke, Kit Roberts and B Cliff

Right: Batian under full sail (photo: Dave Clarke, from the cross-trees)

211

Batian in heavy weather in mid-Atlantic

Each day we recorded plus or minus 100 miles all very comfortable with no anxiety. It was wonderful to be in mid-Atlantic and feel utterly confident, secure and able to handle anything that came our way.

On our twenty-fifth day at sea we sighted the mountain Pico in the Azores and on our twenty-sixth day we sailed into Horta; at 06.30 we secured to the main quay. Dave Clarke left us there and flew back to the U.K. Sheila wished to complete the voyage back to Gibraltar but we first rested for twenty days to enjoy the delightful Azores and its people. I write "rested", but Sheila reminds me that she was upset and angry when, apparently, I berated her to "stop all this sleeping" when we entered a yacht race from Horta to the neighbouring island of São Jorge and back. Amongst all those white, plastic yachts we were second to last, beating only a French wooden boat which had sailed from Jamaica "at our pace". From the wonderful people on

São Jorge we were presented with a large pot of honey and a huge cheese, for taking part in the race.

At Horta I contacted a man in England who had also been in Government service in Kenya. Ian Gibson was a veterinary officer and had lived and worked not far from me in the same district near Mt Kenya when I was employed in the agricultural department. He had climbed Nelion on Mt Kenya with me and I was aware that he was also ex-Royal Navy. Armed with a sextant, he flew to the Azores to join us for the sail back to Portugal.

It took us two days to sail through the Azore islands to leave them eventually on our stern as we headed eastwards. Out in the open sea we experienced two gales of Force 8, when we used the storm jib and trysail. Ian had lost an eye in Kenya, when a robber had attacked him and consequently he had some difficulty using his sextant. He steadfastly persevered, but his results seldom corresponded with mine. I also saw that he was rather unsteady on the foredeck, so I suggested that it would be better if I handled all the sail changing alone. As a larger, heavier man, Sheila and I would have had great difficulty in recovering him or even moving him if he had slipped or suffered an injury. He was good to have on board, however, and dutifully stood his watches.

After nine days we picked up Cape St Vincent light off the port bow at 01.45 one morning and were abeam the cape by 08.00, in a very heavy sea, once again under storm jib and trysail. It took us all that day to sail alongside the Portuguese southern coast and at 19.00 we were safely secured at Vilamoura marina, where Ian subsequently left us to return to his family in the U.K. We had chosen to make our landfall in Vilamoura to meet up again with Pat, the Australian, and his wife, Judith, to tell them how the boat had behaved. Sadly, we learned that he had died soon after we had departed nine months previously and Judith was in the process of selling their boat. The following day, Sheila and I put to sea again and the two of us sailed the boat to Gibraltar, briefly calling in at El Rompido in southern Spain en route.

Since I had work to do in England, I decided to leave *Batian* in Gibraltar for the winter. Sheila, with no plans of her own and no desire to leave, offered to stay on the boat to look after it and do some maintenance while she lived on board. I was very grateful for her offer and to have someone to tend to the mooring lines and keep the boat safe. On my return four months later with the intention of returning the boat to Corsica, I was amazed to see all the work she had done. All the woodwork had been varnished and the interior re-upholstered (see opposite).

The boat was ready for sea and taking on a young man who wanted to get into the Mediterranean, we left on the first good westerly wind. We rested briefly at Aguilas, southern Spain, before continuing to Cartagena, again for a brief visit, then to

Mahon on Minorca. Using mainly meridian altitude sights of the sun, we navigated back to Corsica and through the Straits of Bonifacio to Porto Vecchio, the port we had left nineteen months previously. It had been a wonderful and satisfying experience, with happy crew on all the different passages ably playing their parts and thankful for the opportunity to sail on

Batian. The success of the voyage was due, in no small part, to all those who helped, in particular Sheila, who was there for the whole time. Sadly, she later announced that she had lost her nerve and would never sail again.

I continued to live on the yacht in Corsica but after a while, the urge to go to sea returned and I planned another voyage.

Chapter 13

The Canaries

To Gibraltar ...

My nephew Charles, from New Zealand visited me in Corsica when he was sixteen and with him came a letter from my sister, Valerie, asking me to "teach him how to sail and to climb!" He was already into serious cycling (he was in his school's racing team), had ambitions for the Tour de France and avidly read cycling magazines whilst he was with me.

Together with a French colleague of mine we climbed on Punta Diamante in Corsica and sailed whenever we could but he did not seem to be too attracted to either sport. He returned to New Zealand to continue his education and periodically visited me again in England; we toured Norway on cycles on one visit.

I had in mind taking the yacht to New Zealand by way of the Panama Canal and South Pacific and suggested this voyage to Charles. He came over to England in the autumn wishing to work in Europe for the winter sports season and eventually left by public transport for Chamonix to search for employment. Already a linguist, fluent in French and German, he soon found a job. My plan was to start the voyage by sailing *Batian* from Corsica to the Canary Islands during the winter where he would join me in the spring for the voyage to New Zealand after his winter season in the Alps.

For crew for the initial voyage to Gibraltar I was joined by John Leach, who also owned a wooden boat in Corsica, Stephano, an Italian, keen to sail on *Batian* and Ann, a nurse from Leeds.

217

We had a disastrous start. On the second day out we sailed into a sudden Force 10 storm and were caught with too much sail up. In seconds our Genoa was ripped to pieces and we ran into Mahon on Minorca for repairs. We had also taken on a lot of water and it was necessary to haul the boat out to find the problem. We discovered a number of leaking seams that had sprung in the gale and I had to engage a Spanish boat builder to recaulk some of the hull. With an estimated three weeks out of the water, John and Stephano had to leave me to it.

Batian hauled out in Minorca to find leaking seams and re-caulk

Once the boat was repaired I was joined by Peter, a young student from Ripon in Yorkshire and together again with Ann from Leeds, we put to sea. Ann was chronically seasick, as she had been on the initial leg, and once more was completely incapacitated. We reached Gibraltar where I hunted for further crew. A young engineer, Alan, who had cycled all the way from England to search for a crewing position for the Atlantic appeared on the jetty and impressed by his cycling, I took him on. I hesitated about taking Ann further but, having resigned from her work in Leeds and also rented out her house, she was anxious to continue, confidently saying that different seasickness tablets could overcome the problem.

...Madeira ...

We left in fairly heavy weather and she was soon incapacitated again and on her bunk. As we made our way westward to Madeira I became very concerned as her condition deteriorated to the point when she asked if she could be transferred to any passing ship! Not only had we not seen any other ships, but I felt it would be a real imposition to ask a captain to stop and take on a sea-sick passenger. With no food being served to them, Alan and Peter also became rather agitated at having to make their own meals and Alan in particular expressed a lack of confidence in my navigating without satellite assistance; I also caught him having whispered conversations with young Peter at the foot of the mainmast, clearly "ganging up against the skipper"!

In spite of the concerns, Porto Santos duly appeared dead on the bow after eight days at sea, and with great relief we anchored in the large harbour there. A doctor came on board and examined Ann, who was seriously dehydrated and very ill. I attempted to get a flight home for her but was unsuccessful. After a week in harbour she, yet again, wanted to try a different remedy and to continue on the voyage. It was having such a bad effect upon morale that I was reluctant to take her further. I did feel, however, that on the passage to the Canaries in the south, with the prevailing westerlies more or less on the starboard beam or quarter, the motion of *Batian* would be considerably more gentle than during the beating we had done to get to Madeira. So we took to the sea again! Sure enough, as soon as the boat started to roll, Ann took to her bunk with chronic seasickness yet again. In four days, however, we reached Gran Canaria, where I arranged a flight for her back to the U.K.

... and the Canaries

At Las Palmas, the harbour was completely full of ARC (Atlantic Rally for Cruisers) boats waiting for their start in the rally, so we were obliged to anchor in the bay. Alan and Peter wished to go ashore and accepted a lift there from a passing dinghy, whilst I remained on board to work on *Batian*. They said they would find their own way back on board later on. I retired early and at some time in the night heard them come back on board. Early in the morning a wind sprang up, and I was awakened by the noise of a boat bumping our top-sides; on hurriedly reaching the cockpit I found a fisherman's wooden boat tied to us. Awakening Alan and Peter from their inebriated state I was informed that they had "borrowed" (*their* word) the boat in order to get back on board and would return it in the morning. Knowing that, as captain, I would be held responsible for the theft (*my* word) of the fisherman's boat, I got them out of bed to return it immediately, which they did with me following in our dinghy to fetch them back on board. At a more or less silent breakfast in the morning they announced that they would be leaving to join another boat with a skipper who was "less of a bastard"! I was pleased to hear this news but my sympathies were with young Peter, who had shaped up well before being "contaminated" by Alan who, of course, I was pleased to see the back of.

I remained at Las Palmas for a while before eventually sailing *Batian* to Puerto Mogan in the south of Gran Canaria – a more suitable place to spend the rest of the winter and to prepare the yacht for the voyage to New Zealand. During the winter I made a brief visit to Chamonix to meet with my nephew Charles and some of his friends there. At a meeting with them all in a café, I talked of our plans to sail *Batian* to

Sailing Batian to Puerto Mogan under cruising chute

New Zealand and suggested to Charles that he might like to invite and select two of his friends to join us as crew. They all appeared to be enthusiastic and I left it to him to do the selecting. I returned to Puerto Mogan to await the end of the winter sports season in Chamonix.

At Puerto Mogan, Gran Canaria

In mid-April Charles duly arrived at the port and shortly afterwards, two young French friends of his. Both called Olivier, one was a professional chef and I hence thought immediately a good choice, imagining French cuisine on the high ocean; but the seriousness and demeanour of the other impressed me more. None of them had much sailing experience so we set about a training exercise. After a few days I was somewhat taken aback when Charles called me aside one morning to inform me that they were all getting bored (at that time we had been weather-bound in port). In spite of a poor weather forecast I replied that we would have a trial sail across to Tenerife the following morning. When all was ready, with instructions how to cast off, handle ropes, hoist sails, etc., etc., we duly left and very soon hit the confused seas that run between Tenerife and Gran Canaria. Olivier (the chef) was soon down on his bunk with seasickness as *Batian* started the customary roll. We had cause to reef the mainsail and I struggled alone at the foot of the mainmast whilst trying to teach the procedure. It was at that stage that I wished I had taken on climbers, who at least are used to handling ropes! All in all, I was somewhat disappointed at our first foray to sea, for I didn't sense much enthusiasm. This was exacerbated when, on anchoring off Los Christianos, where it was my intention to go through where things had gone wrong, the only comment was that they wished to use the dinghy to go ashore and visit the bars ... to which I reluctantly agreed. Alone in the lovely anchorage, I reflected on my own apprenticeship and the cost and determined effort I had to undergo to learn how to sail. Here, they were getting it all free on a lovely boat and not showing much appreciation! I decided we would have a further trial and sail to La Gomera, the next island, on the following morning.

We left at 07.00 and sailed to San Sebastien on La Gomera where, once again, the preference was for the bars in the evening rather than practicing reefing or discussing handling the yacht in the weather we could expect in the ocean. Overnight, I reflected on what I would be taking on; I had exhausted myself trying to teach and impart enthusiasm into these young men and the back injury I had suffered in the aircraft accident was limiting the physical effort I myself could put into maintaining and sailing *Batian*.

At La Gomera. Left to right: Olivier, Charles (my nephew), Olivier (the chef)

In the morning, after they asked what we would be doing that day, I announced that we would be sailing the yacht back to Mogan on Gran Canaria and cancelling the planned passage to New Zealand. On the return voyage I became exhausted again with none of the young men learning anything. They departed on their various ways and slowly I came to the conclusion that the boat was getting too much for me. Owning, sailing and maintaining an elderly wooden boat is more than a hobby; it is a passion and a heavy commitment which I had enjoyed for ten years. Very reluctantly, back at Puerto Mogan, I came to an inevitable decision.

The end for *Batian*

I decided to put the yacht up for sale in *Classic Boat* magazine but it took over eighteen months before interested prospective buyers came to Mogan to inspect *Batian*. During that time, and in between visits to my property in the Yorkshire Dales, I lived on the yacht and continued to maintain it in the consistently high standard to which I was used. Indeed, it was a great pleasure to climb both the main and mizzen masts every three months to treat the lovely Oregon pine, from which they were constructed with a special Norwegian oil (Deks Olje). Varnishing the mahogany coach roof and deck fittings also gave me much pleasure.

An Irishman, claiming to be a master mariner showed interest particularly as the asking price was periodically reduced in *Classic Boat* magazine. With further haggling I took him and his companions out for a trial sail. I was somewhat surprised, bearing in mind his experience, at his refusal of my offer to allow him to take the helm to handle the yacht out of its berth, or return it back there; similarly for the sail handling. I was also surprised when, during a demonstration of how to climb the masts and how to get into the very constricted engine bay, he informed me that he would be doing neither! Nevertheless, he eventually bought *Batian* and I very reluctantly handed it over. Some months later a 'phone call informed me that I had sold a "leaking boat"! I then learned that the boat had been taken out of the water for anti-fouling and had been left in the hot Canarian sun for some time without protection or hosing the hull down with water each evening, as is necessary for a wooden hull in the tropics. Understandably, the seams had opened with the heat.

With a crew of three elderly men, *Batian* was taken to Cork in Ireland, where I saw it once again a year later on a cycling holiday there, lying forlorn against a jetty. Seven years later I saw it advertised for sale, again in *Classic Boat* and berthed in southern Spain. The advert described it as "faithfully maintained in very good condition, renovated and fully geared, ready for serious sailing." In those seven years I had missed the ownership of *Batian* terribly, and it had affected me so much that friends had accused me of being withdrawn! I became very enthused again and felt confident that my back injury, then giving me less pain would allow me to sail again. Full of hope, with prospective crew and carrying my sextant, I went to Almeria on the south coast of Spain with the intention of buying it back and sailing to my friends in Corsica, where they had already organised a berth for the yacht.

I had difficulty in locating the boat but eventually I found the agent with whom it was advertised. The agent's first words were, "Are you ready for a shock", for she, a middle-aged lady very knowledgeable on wooden boats, was aware that I was the previous owner who had carefully nurtured the boat. Shock indeed, for she took me to the yacht and I saw immediately that it was in a dreadful state! The servo rudder of the Aries wind vane, removable by a simple thumb screw had been left in the water and was covered in barnacles, as was the rest of the hull. The caulking in the hull seams was spewing out and the engine controls were completely seized with rust. The two lovely Oregon Pine masts had been painted with brown paint. It appeared that no maintenance had been done for a very long time. Worse still, neither the cooking stove nor heads (toilets) had apparently ever been cleaned since my ownership! I estimated that it would take six months hard work to get the yacht into a sea-worthy state. Thoroughly disheartened, I felt unable to take it on again and I left *Batian* to its fate.

Writing to my sailor friends in Corsica to explain that I would not be returning with *Batian*, I received the following comments: "J'ai bien reçu ta lettre. Pauvre Batian. Achète toi un bon bateau tout en plastique inox et alu." In my previous time with them in Corsica they had always been rather critical of the work in which *Batian* involved me and even then had always considered plastic a better option for me.

With the pedigree as a Colin Archer and character *Batian* had ably demonstrated in my time at sea in all weathers, I could not possibly entertain their advice.

It was, indeed, a sad end to sailing adventures ...

Chapter 14

St Helena

... Well, perhaps not quite the end for a work colleague of mine from the Agricultural Department in Kenya was offered the position of Agricultural Officer in Saint Helena some years ago and his letters to me were always full of enthusiasm for the island. Meeting with him again by chance in Corsica five years ago he reckoned that there are three places in the world worth living in: Kenya; Corsica; and Saint Helena. As a result of his sentiments and with its fascinating position in the South Atlantic, I had planned to sail to Saint Helena whilst still owning *Batian*.

In November of 2001, however, I had a sudden opportunity to participate in a yacht race from Cape Town to Saint Helena and I hurriedly flew down there. Regrettably I missed the start of the race but I did manage to get on the "chase" boat sailing a day later. This was the Royal Mail ship *St Helena*, the last ocean-going Royal Mail ship and which sails regularly from Cardiff to Cape Town *via* the Canaries, Ascension Island and St Helena. After weaving our way through the fleet of yachts at sea we reached St Helena where I disembarked and the ship duly continued on to Ascension Island. This gave me fourteen days on the island to await the yachts and then hopefully get a berth for the return to Cape Town.

Small and beautiful, the island is set in the tropical South Atlantic approximately 15°55' South, 5° 40' West, 1,500 miles northwest of Cape Town and over 1,000 west of Angola. It is an island of contrasts, from multi-coloured ridges of wind-eroded desert to emerald hillsides, soft pasture and lush vegetation-filled valleys. A coastline of magnificent 1,000-foot high bronze-coloured cliffs almost all round the island has been carved over centuries by pounding Atlantic rollers.

It is perhaps not surprising that the early navigators in their search for a sea route to India missed the island for they hugged the coastline and only after the Cape was first rounded (by Bartholomew Dias in 1487), paving the way for the eventual sea route did ships venture further out to sea. In 1502 the Portuguese Admiral João do Nova on his return voyage from India discovered the island where he left goats, game birds, fruit and herbs for the Portuguese to then use as a secret watering and victualling base. The island was uninhabited but in 1513 an unfortunate Portuguese sailor was left alone there for punishment and he hence became the first lonely inhabitant.

It was not until 1588 that the English found the island where Captain Thomas Cavendish called there on the homeward leg of his round-the-world voyage. Thereafter both the English and the Dutch frequently called for fresh water and fruit. The English took possession of the island in 1659 and with its prime location on the trade route back from the East Indies they established the English East India Company and built the first permanent settlement at James Valley. They also developed St Helena into a true fortress with all the fortifications guarded by batteries. By 1723 the population of the island was over one thousand, half of whom were slaves. The eighteenth-century prosperity which the island enjoyed due to its location on the trade route greatly diminished in 1869 with the first steamships and the opening of the Suez Canal. The only industry that has provided the island with substantial income was the production of New Zealand flax which started in 1870, the fibre being used to make string and sacking. At its height, the crop covered nearly 1,400 hectares. With the introduction of synthetic fibres the industry collapsed in 1965 and at present tourism would appear to be giving an increasing income.

Clearly it is not an easy place to get to and even when you get there the island is not easy to get ON to. There is no harbour and ships have to lie at anchor in the Atlantic off Jamestown. Passengers have to be ferried ashore in small boats to a jetty where with the usual Atlantic swell stepping ashore can be hazardous. Whilst I was there the *Q.E.II* arrived with seven hundred passengers but with a huge swell the captain rightly refused to let any of his passengers ashore with a resultant sad loss of income to the islanders (called Saints). On our arrival there we were instructed how to get into a small boat and how to wait for the right moment when stepping ashore. Some passengers were clearly alarmed and as an alternative were offered "The Aerial Lift". I immediately thought that it must be a helicopter but no it was not. Passengers are asked to stand in the luggage cage which is then hoisted by the ship's crane from the deck into the small boat below. Arriving at the jetty, the jetty crane then lifts the cage off. There are plans to build an airport with the pros and cons being discussed at length, but one cannot help but feel that this wonderful haven will be spoiled. Most Saints, however, appear to feel that provided it is kept as a small enterprise with numbers of tourists restricted, the island will benefit.

The island has had many famous visitors but the most famous resident was Napoleon Bonaparte taken there after his defeat at Waterloo. He was perhaps the cause of the description "this uneventful rock: the most isolated, the least known, the least accessible and the best suited for use as a prison." He was resident there at Longwood House from 1815 to his death on the island in 1821. Longwood House, Briars Pavilion (his first residence) and The Valley of the Tomb are all now French properties and are tourist attractions. Napoleon's body was buried in the Valley of the Tomb where it remained until 1840 when his remains were exhumed and taken to France. The Emperor's body lies at rest in Les Invalides in Paris as in his will he had written that "I wish my remains to rest beside the Seine, in the midst of the French people whom I love so much."

Saint Helena can best be described as an oasis of peace away from the pressures of modern living. Jamestown, the capital and seat of government is a legacy of the East India Company with a museum, small hotels and shops. It is blessed with warm-hearted friendly people, a pleasant climate, a fascinating heritage with early military fortifications in abundance, spectacular scenery and superb wild walks.

During my stay there all the yachts arrived after good passages with the following southeast trade winds. It occurred to me that the sailing would not be quite so easy into headwinds on the return passage but searching for a berth I found to my amazement that the plan was to put the yachts on the Royal

Mail ship *St Helena* for the return. Now that's the way to do it for ageing sailors and with the yachts and sailors safely on board we had a very Merry Christmas at sea and a very easy passage back to Cape Town.

Above: The yachts were loaded onto the "St Helena" for the return

Right: Approaching Table Mountain and Cape Town with the yachts on board, and an easy passage back!

Chapter 15

Epilogue

With advancing age and accentuated back problems giving more severe pain, it became increasingly difficult to consider further adventures.

The cottage I bought, whilst still owning and sailing *Batian* lies in the Yorkshire Dales National Park in Littondale, a delightful valley branching off to the west from Upper Wharfedale near Kilnsey Crag. The river Skirfare runs down Littondale and joins the river Wharfe close to the crag. The Skirfare is directly in front of Elbeck Cottage, my property and provides a wonderful vibrant quiet haven. As with many of the Yorkshire dales, Littondale can be very wet. Indeed when I first came up here in 1996, I commented on the amount of rain to Dennis Lund, my neighbouring farmer. "Well," he said, "if you're freetened of o'bit of watter you shouldn't be coming up 'ere." On further enquiring where I had come from, I told

Dennis Lund outside his home at East Garth

Top: Castle Farm in 1905 before conversion to three properties, Elbeck Cottage (left), Elbeck Barn (centre) and Elbeck House

Above: Elbeck Cottage with River Skirfare in front

him about Africa and growing tea. Straight to the point again he remarked, "You won't grow any tea up 'ere."

Elbeck Cottage adjoins two other properties, Elbeck Barn and Elbeck House in one long building at one time called Castle Farm and last farmed as such by the Coates family in the 1950s. Elbeck House was always the main habitation for the resident farmer with the barn in the middle used as such and Elbeck Cottage on the end used as a calf-rearing and milking parlour. The Coates family ceased farming in 1961 and sold the whole building to a Mr Holmes, an owner of a packaging firm in Bradford. He, in turn, sold it quite quickly on to Mr Bendalow, a parliamentarian who converted the calf-rearing parlour into a cottage ... Elbeck Cottage for the use of his elderly mother, some time in 1965-70. The property then changed ownership again and Mr Walker, a professional artist and sculptor, moved in with his family to Elbeck House and he also bought the adjoining barn and used it as his studio and workshop. Elbeck Cottage, then converted, was sold separately as a private residence to a Mr Rushby and there were other owners before I purchased it in 1996. In the meantime Mr Walker at Elbeck House sold the centre building barn, to Mr Oldham, in 1980, who then converted it into a private residence now known as Elbeck Barn. He owned and lived in it with his wife Mary for almost twenty years before it changed hands again – three times in five years during my residence at the cottage at the end of the building.

Dennis Lund's farm – East Garth – lies to the south of the Elbeck complex and on his land, four hundred yards up the hillside from his house a spring of water exits from the side of the hill (called a foss in the Dales). I was quite surprised to learn that the property which I was interested in buying, drew water from Dennis' foss together with nine other properties in the village by an ingenious system of tapping into the source at the hillside by a pipe followed by four sediment tanks. The supply is then piped down the hillside by gravity alone and crosses the river Skirfare, from whence the nine properties draw their supply – all gravity fed with good pressure. Being acquainted with similar systems in Africa, I was soon elected to become Chairman of the Foss Water Partnership on becoming resident of Elbeck Cottage. This involves holding periodic meetings with the partners, looking after and maintaining the system and also cleaning the four sediment tanks by siphoning out the sediment tanks from time to time. It is preferable to install a filter and ultra-violet treatment plant at the inlet point to each property in order to purify the water which can contain harmful organisms. Coming from Africa

The foss on the hillside

and being quite used to using water from a doubtful supply, I initially scorned installing a treatment point at my property, as did Dennis and other long-term neighbours. At an early meeting of the Foss Water Partners and introducing a new partner on the sale of one of the properties, the new partner commented on the quality of the water whereupon Dennis soon gave his opinion – "Well," he said, "I've supped it all me life and there's nowt wrong wi' me."

The river Skirfare flows over porous limestone rock and as a consequence in light rainfall and usually for most of the summer, certain stretches dry out. One of these stretches lies immediately in front of my property where there is a "sink hole". It then becomes an interesting dry river bed. After a few hours of steady rain upstream, the river starts to flow, sometimes quite gradually but usually by a wall of water rushing down, rather like the renowned Severn Bore near Bristol, then it soon becomes a roaring torrent eight feet deep or so, with a waterfall immediately in front of my property and it can rise onto the lawn. When it is in spate, canoeists sometimes come down the river and shoot the waterfall (overleaf). Also after a lengthy drought period tree branches are often swept down and not long ago a whole ash tree floated down. I collect the wood from the river and cut and burn it in an open fire to heat my house. The ash tree lasted a whole winter! I get great pleasure in sawing and splitting wood provided by the river and it certainly keeps me fit. Littondale is also an excellent quite valley for cycling and it is a pleasure to be able to cycle or walk direct from my house without first having to drive somewhere by car.

A local resident in Arncliffe, aware of our crocodile encounter years ago commented that there are no crocodiles up here! Since the river dries out, there are no trout either but there are below at Arncliffe where it flows continuously and where fishing permits are available at the Falcon Inn, Arncliffe. Most of the properties I lived in whilst in Africa had separate guest accommodation as small buildings, usually in the gardens. I was surprised to find that Elbeck Cottage had just such guest accommodation constructed above the garage which is a separate building behind the property. When I first inspected the house and saw the separate guest accommodation, it reminded me so much of Africa that it influenced my decision to purchase. With access to the property running in front of the two adjoining properties, another criterion of mine was met – that of security. At the time of purchase I owned the ketch *Batian*, then moored in Corsica and I was away on the boat for lengthy periods. Security was hence an important criterion for me and Elbeck Cottage met that aspect. Accordingly I went ahead with the purchase in 1996 and have now lived in the valley for sixteen years. Although, at first, it took some time for me to settle, it has proved ideal for my lifestyle. It is reckoned that once you have lived in Africa, it never gets out of your blood, and that has certainly been the case for me. Knowing something of my past, the Proprietor of the Falcon Inn in Arncliffe, Robin Miller, queried how on earth I could settle and live in the quiet dale of Littondale after such an adventurous lifestyle. I originally responded, "With some difficulty", but it has not been a problem for me. As I did in Africa, I can live close to nature as, of course, the local farmers do and I can easily identify with them. For the first few years of residence here and whilst I was still fit, it was a pleasure to help with sheepwork and haymaking. I regard it as a privilege to be able to live amongst the Littondale farmers and residents in this delightful valley.

Canoeists on the Skirfare

241

Acknowledgements

I was fortunate enough to have wonderful understanding parents who backed all my exploits without question. My father worked in the wool trade in Bradford and my mother, my two sisters and myself were his whole reason for living! He kept himself active and apart from his garden had few other hobbies. He himself had to look after a family at the tender age of fourteen when his father died and he was sent out to work and care for his mother and four younger siblings of two brothers and two sisters. His aim in life was that his children would have a more prosperous and educated life than his. He dearly wished to be a teacher but circumstances would never allow it.

My mother also came from an even larger family of seven sisters and four brothers. They were all happy smiling people, caring for each other and amongst the many aunts, uncles and cousins, I never heard a wrong word. They were a joy to grow up with.

Quite simply, of all the people I have met, my father was the nicest man I have ever come across. He was self-educated with delightful compassion and impeccable manners.

When I resigned from the WHO in order to return home from Africa to assist with elderly ailing parents, I soon noticed that my mother had dementia. I commented to my father that her repeated comments must be nerve-wracking. He looked me straight in the eyes and said, "Looking after YOUR mother … " (he did not say "MY wife", by which he meant that it was my responsibility also) "... is not a task, it is a privilege." I felt considerably humbled for what finer words can a man utter? Both he, my mother and also lately my elder sister passed from life whilst I held them in my arms. What poignant memories to be with them for their last breath on earth.

Most of my friends have constantly told me to write a book. It has been an arduous task and I can only hope that it gives some enjoyment.

It is dedicated to those who have participated in the events; those who have climbed with me, flown with me and sailed with me and in all cases put their trust in me. I have needed help in compiling the book and in particular the computer skills and guidance of Howard Wilson has provided that. It could not have been finalised without his help and I am very grateful to him.

List of Illustrations

South face of Mount Kenya
Beaver take-off on Kaieteur Falls, Guyana   Front Cover

At the helm of Batian on the east cost of Corsica   Back Cover

B Cliff and R Baillie on Table Mountain   Frontispiece

Chapter 1   Mountaineering
Eight agricultural students   23
Seven young men and a motor-cycle combination   25
Climbing coconut tree   30
Mount Kenya from rice research station   34

Chapter 2   Mount Kenya
Don Gray at the top of Mackinder's Chimney   38
Amongst the giant heather on Mt Kenya   46
Mt Kenya from the south   47
Top of Firmin's Tower   52
West Face of Mt Kenya   55
Looking down Heim glacier - moonlight   56
B Cliff on the Forel glacier   56
R Baillie at the top of Forel glacier   56
Thompson's Flake   59
East face of Nelion and Thompson's Flake   60
Learning glacier flying   63

Chapter 3   Nelion's northeast pillar and east face
North face of Mt Kenya   67
Our camp on Krapf col   68
Near start of northeast pillar of Nelion   69
Our first bivouac   71
D Rutowitz on second day - two tents can be seen   72
D Rutowitz on summit after 2½ days   73
Top Hut, Mt Kenya   75
With the Austrians at Top Hut   76
The Austrians examine our gear   76
East face   78
East face and part of northeast pillar   79
H Klier on East face   80
S Aeberli on East face   80
B Cliff on East face   80
H Klier on East face   80

Chapter 4   Kenya Independence
             Austin Gypsy on Mt Kenya   85
             John Hull on South face   86

Chapter 5   Mount Kilimanjaro to Mount Kenya in under 24 hours
             R Baillie and B Cliff on Atlantic Crack   91
             Jaguar XK150   93
             Bivouac on Mt Kilimanjaro   94
             B Cliff on Kili summit   94
             R Baillie and B Cliff on Mt Kilimanjaro   95
             B Cliff running in forest   96
             R Baillie on Batian summit   99

Chapter 7   Crocodile Encounter
             The Canoe   110
             First trial   110
             Crocodiles   111

Chapter 8   Adventures in Aviation 1
             Maralal airstrip and horses   123
             Naibor Enkeju   124
             B Cliff on Naibor Enkeju   124
             R Baillie on Naibor Enkeju   124
             Aircraft accident   127
             Aircraft accident   127

Chapter 9   Adventures in Aviation 2
             De Havilland Rapide   135
             The Red Devils   135
             Spraying sugar cane in a Piper Pawnee in Guyana 138
             Beaver plus canoe   140
             Over tropical forest   141
             Kaieteur Falls   143
             Beaver take-off from falls   144
             Colour of falls   144
             Canoe on Beaver float   147
             Bush jetty   147
             Narrow river   148
             Branch over Potaro River   150
             Girder bridge on Garroway Stream   153
             Right-angled bend   153
             View of Beaver from bridge   153
             Beaver take-off   155

Chapter 10   Adventures in Aviation 3
             Piper Seneca in Seychelles   158
             Seneca at Ngoro Ngoro   159
             Programme area & West Africa   163

Chapter 10   Adventures in Aviation 3 (cont.)
Farmer with River Blindness   163
Treatment of breeding site by helicopter   163
Examination of river breeding site   165
Turbo Thrush special   165
Addressing the crowd   165
River spraying, Hughes 500D   166
River spraying, Hughes 500C   166
Pangalet, Bill Riley and B Cliff   170
B Cliff with radio   172
Accident on Comoe River   175

Chapter 11   Sailing Adventures
Sunstream   183
Batian   189
Batian   191

Chapter 12   The Atlantic
Batian saloon   196
Aries wind vane   199
We caught fish   200
Sextant navigating   202
Batian in Demerara   204
Batian in Barbados   209
Batian saloon - three men   211
Batian under full sail   211
Batian in heavy weather   212
Upholstery and varnish, Batian saloon   215

Chapter 13   The Canaries
Batian in Minorca for caulking   218
Cruising chute   221
Batian in Puerto Mogan   222
Batian in La Gomera   224

Chapter 14   St Helena
Yachts on "St Helena"   233
Approaching Table Mountain   233

Chapter 15   Epilogue
Dennis Lund at East Garth   235
Castle Farm in 1905   236
Elbeck Cottage and River Skirfare   236
The Foss   238
Canoeists in the Skirfare   241
Canoeists in the Skirfare   241